W9-AWK-608

# WRITING

## A Fact and Fun Book

BY Amanda Lewis

ILLUSTRATIONS BY Heather Collins

ORIGINAL LETTERING BY AMANDA LEWIS

Addison-Wesley Publishing Company

Reading, Massachusetts ○ Menlo Park, California ○ New York
Don Mills, Ontario ○ Wokingham, England ○ Amsterdam ○ Bonn
Sydney ○ Singapore ○ Tokyo ○ Madrid ○ San Juan
Paris ○ Seoul ○ Milan ○ Mexico City ○ Taipei

For my mother, who taught me how to see

•

## ACKNOWLEDGEMENTS

No book is an island, and this one has certainly had a lot of support and encouragement from many people whose contributions remain invisible. I am grateful for support from the Ontario Arts Council, and for the help and information provided by Gary Lewis, Eleanor Scott, Irene Aubrey and Freda Taylor at the National Library of Canada, Jane Carr at the British Library, Ruth Harrington at Blissymbolics Communication International, the Bibliothèque Nationale, the Pierpont Morgan Library, the Bodleian Library, the Canadian Pulp and Paper Association, the Recycling Council of Ontario, Unicef Canada, the Canadian National Institute for the Blind, the Canadian Organization for Development through Education and the Canadian Children's Book Centre.

I am especially in debt to the wonderful staff at the Perth Union Library who responded to my bizarre requests with enthusiasm and creativity, as well as to Virgil Burnett and Nancy Lou Patterson at the University of Waterloo Fine Arts Department, who started me on this road in the first place. Thanks also to Dr. Ka Bo Tsang of the Far Eastern Department of the Royal Ontario Museum for her advice on Chinese writing, and for rendering the Chinese specimens.

A big thank-you hug to the students of Cherrywood Alternative School and Brooke Valley School for helping me to develop these activities; and to my own brilliant mark-makers Xan, Maddy and Lewis for being my best teachers.

I am very grateful to everyone at Kids Can Press for supporting me with such warmth and enthusiasm; to Michael Solomon, designer *par excellence*, who allowed me to pick his brain on many occasions; to Heather Collins for her inspired and well-researched illustrations; and to my compassionate editor, Val Wyatt, who was right beside me all the time—holding my hand through the magic of the fax machine.

And finally to Tim, my most devoted critic, without whose patience and support this book would have remained only a twinkle in my eye.

---

*Library of Congress Cataloging-in-Publication Data*

Lewis, Amanda.
  Writing, a fact and fun book / by Amanda Lewis : illustrations by Heather Collins : original lettering by Amanda Lewis.
    p.  cm.
  Includes index.
  Summary: Discusses the history of writing, the development of pens and pencils, how books are published, and how to write stories, journals, and articles.
    ISBN 0-201-63236-5
    1. Writing—Juvenile literature. 2. Authorship—Juvenile literature. 3. Books—Juvenile literature. [1. Writing. 2. Authorship. 3. Books.] I. Collins, Heather, ill. II. Title.
Z40.L48 1992
411—dc20                                   92-2363
                                              CIP
                                              AC

1 2 3 4 5 6 7 8 9–AL–95949392
First printing, August 1992

Text copyright © 1992 by Amanda Lewis
Illustrations copyright © 1992 by Heather Collins
Calligraphy, lettering and pictograms copyright © 1992 by Amanda Lewis
Chinese writing copyright © 1992 by Ka Bo Tsang

All rights reserved. No part of this publication may be reproduced, stored in a retrieval system, or transmitted, in any form or by any means, electronic, mechanical, photocopying, recording, or otherwise, without the prior written permission of the publisher. Printed in the United States of America.

Neither the Publisher nor the Author shall be liable for any damage which may be caused or sustained as a result of conducting any of the activities in this book without specifically following instructions, conducting the activities without proper supervision, or ignoring the cautions contained in the book.

Originally published in Canada by Kids Can Press, Ltd., of Toronto, Ontario.

Edited by Valerie Wyatt
Designed by Michael Solomon
Set in 15-point Garamond Antiqua by Compeer Typographic Services Limited

Addison-Wesley books are available at special discounts for bulk purchases by schools and other organizations. For more information, please contact:
Special Markets Department
Addison-Wesley Publishing Company
Reading, MA 01867
(617) 944-3700 x 2431

 Text stock contains over 50% recycled paper

# CONTENTS

SARA

Laudа

ΕΥΟΣΙΑΝ
ΝΕΙΝΑΙ
ΙΤΕΜΒΟ
ΑΤΑΗΙ

BVLL
R

# INTRODUCTION

**D**O YOU remember learning how to write — how exciting it felt to make marks on the page that meant *you*, your name? How proud you felt at finally making a perfect S? Have you ever doodled with your letters, making them fancy, or extra special? Then this book is for you.

Writing is a kind of magic. It allows you to share your thoughts with anyone who can read. Maybe your ideas will be read by people hundreds of years from now! Reading other people's writing lets you travel to other places and other times. And when you read writing you can learn things — how to make a chocolate cake, raise a rabbit or build a glider. Knowledge that is written down is there for everyone to use.

But how did writing start? There are more than 9000 languages in the world today, but only 300 of them are written. Millions of people carry on their lives and their cultures without writing and have done so for thousands of years. Why, then, did some people, in some places, start to write? Why does writing look the way it does? Where do pens and pencils and paper come from? Because you can read, you can find out the answers to these questions. In this book, you'll also find out:

- how the alphabet comes from an ox and a house
- how to make things to write with (like your own chalk, a feather pen and honey soot ink)
- ideas for writing beautifully (calligraphy) or tastefully (with chocolate pudding!)

There are puzzles to figure out ("What were the last three letters to join the alphabet?") and tips from writers on writing ("Keep a pair of scissors handy"). You'll find out how to do the oldest form of writing (Chinese brush writing), and how one little thought can spread out to millions of strangers. So turn the page and discover the most important story of the last 5000 years, the story of writing.

*...from an ox and a house...?*

IMAGINE your day without reading or writing. You want to visit a friend's house and you've never been there before. She gives you the directions. You can't write, so you have to remember them (was that the second street after the first set of lights or the first street after the second?). When you finally get there, you want to watch some television. But there's no T.V. guide and nobody can remember — was your favorite show on Channel 4 at 5:00 or 5 at 4:00? You decide to make a pizza, but there are no instructions on the box. Without reading and writing in your day, you could get lost, bored and hungry!

Of course if you've got a really good memory, you could remember all of those things. Before there was writing, people had to rely entirely on their memory. For cave dwellers with no television, no radio, no books or magazines, dark nights around the fire could be very long. So people entertained each other by telling stories. Many of the stories were about history — what happened to your great-great-great-great-great-grandfather when he was a boy. The stories were often repeated year

after year, generation after generation. But no one can remember everything all of the time. To help them remember the best stories, cave dwellers painted pictures on their cave walls. These picture memory aids, called mnemonic devices, were the very first stage in developing a writing system.

You've probably used mnemonic devices many times without thinking about it. Have you ever tied a string on your finger to help you to remember something? The string doesn't tell you what to remember, only *to* remember. Or have you shown a friend a photograph or postcard and told the story of what was going on in the photo, where you were, what your day was like, and who you were visiting? The photograph and the postcard are mnemonic devices to help you to remember an experience or a story.

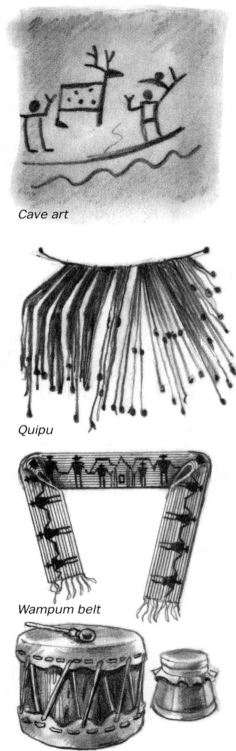

Cave art

Quipu

Wampum belt

Using a picture painted on a cave wall as a mnemonic device was fine — until people wanted to travel or move. Then they needed mnemonic devices that were portable. In Peru, some of the native tribes used a *quipu* (pronounced key-poo) to help them remember tribal stories. This was a series of colored strings and knots that could be worn as a necklace. The different colors of string and the different positions and sizes of the knots all had meaning to the storyteller. They helped him or her remember when and where things happened.

North American Indians used a wampum belt in much the same way. Different colored shells were shaped into beads and woven into a sequence to tell a story. The colors represented different ideas: red was war or anger; black was death or misfortune; white was peace; yellow was gold or tribute. The number of beads used, their color and their order would help the storyteller remember the story.

Drums were another portable mnemonic device. Some tribes found that if they made their story rhyme and told it to the beat of a drum, it was easier to remember. Only the right words would fit at the right time.

Most memorization techniques are based on sound or vision. Hearing a sound like a drum beat or seeing a colored bead can help you to remember. But only the person who has done the memorizing in the first place can tell you the story. If that

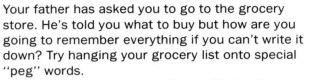

# PEG WORDS

Your father has asked you to go to the grocery store. He's told you what to buy but how are you going to remember everything if you can't write it down? Try hanging your grocery list onto special "peg" words.

First memorize your peg list—it'll stick in your mind because it rhymes. Once you've learned it, you can use the same pegs over and over again for any list.

### Peg List

| | | |
|---|---|---|
| One — bun | four — door | seven — heaven |
| two — shoe | five — hive | eight — gate |
| three — tree | six — sticks | nine — vine |
| | | ten — hen |

Now attach each thing you need to remember to a peg word. For example, say your grocery list included chicken, cereal, lettuce, butter, flour, eggs, porridge, a magazine, apples and a loaf of bread. Peg each word onto your peg list:

One is a chicken eating a bun, two is cereal shaped like a shoe, three is lettuce in a tree, four is butter smeared on the door, five is flour pouring out of a hive, six is eggs broken with sticks, seven is porridge you eat in heaven, eight is a magazine on the gate, nine is apples on a vine, ten is a loaf of bread under a hen.

Make your word pictures as silly as you can. The more ridiculous the image, the easier it is to remember. Once you make all those silly pictures in your head, then you can shorten your list. You'll find it easy to remember: One: chicken; two: cereal; three: lettuce; four: butter; five: flour; six: eggs; seven: porridge; eight: magazine; nine: apples; ten: loaf of bread. Get someone to make up a list for you and impress him or her with how easily you can memorize it.

person isn't around, the story may get completely forgotten.

Some memorization techniques make pictures that other people can "read." The pictures may not tell the whole story, but they give clues that even a stranger can understand. The Dakota Indians made this kind of mnemonic device. It is called Lone Dog's Winter Count and it is a chronicle of 71 winters starting from the year 1800.

A picture of the most important event of each winter was drawn on a buffalo hide. Even if you are not a part of the

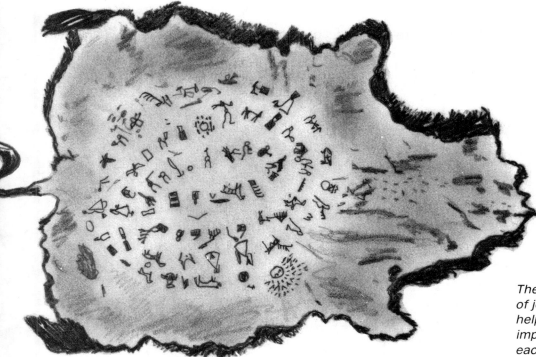

The Dakota Indians kept a kind of journal on a buffalo hide. It helped them to remember an important thing that happened each year.

Dakota tribe, you can guess at many of the events represented and you can follow their sequence. This is a great step forward in the art of writing — for a stranger to be able to understand what you were saying when you are no longer there to say it. For writing does what speech cannot — it goes beyond the barriers of time and space.

## A Picture Is Worth a Thousand Words

Do you ever trade things with your friends? "I'll give you two pieces of gum for that ball." Sometimes, especially if you are trading a lot of things, it's handy to be able to write down your trade. Suppose you didn't know how to read or write. To record your trade deal, you might draw this:

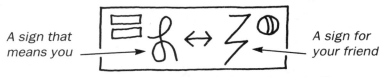

A sign that means you ⟶          ⟵ A sign for your friend

If you ever had an argument about whose ball it was (after the gum was long gone), you could go back and check the deal by looking at the picture.

This is how people used to do business about 10 000 years ago in ancient Mesopotamia (called Iraq today). They made little clay tokens to represent things they wanted to sell. When someone sold some sheep, he would put a sheep token, along with the tokens for the number of sheep sold, into a clay jar. He would then seal the jar so that it couldn't be opened. The jar was then sent along with the person who was delivering the sheep to the buyer. When the sheep arrived, the buyer would break open the jar to check that all of the sheep had been delivered as agreed. Eventually people figured out that they could draw the token shapes on the outside of the jar while the clay was wet, thus saving the need to break a perfectly good jar.

This system could work only if both sides agreed that this token meant sheep: ⊕ and this token meant 100: ●.

You can write a message for your mother saying: ℧∧φ. But unless she knows that ℧ means "I want" and ∧ means "pizza" and φ means "for lunch today," you'll probably go hungry. When people agree on the meaning of abstract drawings like this, they have a code. Only people who understand the code can know the meaning. That's what the traders in Iraq were doing with their tokens. That's how writing got started.

Pictures that people draw to represent objects are called pictograms. Many different cultures used pictograms. Some are really easy to understand; others are unrecognizable until you know the code. For example, illustrated at left is the Egyptian pictogram (or hieroglyph, as Egyptian picture writing is called) for "a person who writes" or "scribe." On the right of the hieroglyph is a palette with two compartments—one for black ink, one for red ink. A bag (center) contains dried colors (pigment), and a holder for pens and brushes is on the left. An Egyptian would have easily recognized these things as tools of the scribe's trade. Can you guess what these other Egyptian pictograms mean? Answers on page 96.

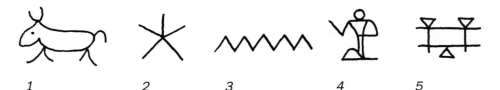

1          2          3          4          5

# A TOKEN OF YOUR AFFECTION

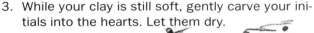

There are lots of shapes that we use to mean different objects or ideas. Probably the most famous is: ♡. Here is a love-ly way to get your message across on Valentine's Day.

**You'll need:**

self-hardening clay or cornstarch clay
a rolling pin
a small heart-shaped cookie cutter or cardboard
to use as a guide
red paint and a paint brush
newspaper or plastic to cover your work area

1. Roll out a slab of clay about 5 mm (¼ inch) thick.
2. Cut out heart shapes, either with a cookie cutter or by cutting around a cardboard heart shape. Make lots of hearts.

3. While your clay is still soft, gently carve your initials into the hearts. Let them dry.

4. Make a clay bowl or a dish to put your hearts in.

5. When the clay is dry, paint the hearts and the bowl red. Then put all the hearts into the bowl and give them to someone you love. He'll "read" your message without you saying a word.

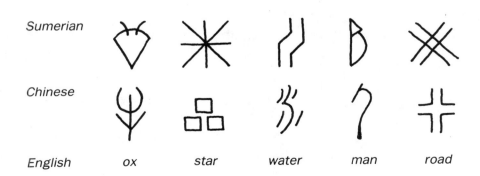

Different groups of people may use different pictograms for the same objects. Here are the ancient Sumerian and ancient Chinese pictograms for the same five words. Notice how similar some are, while others look completely different.

| Sumerian | | | | | |
|---|---|---|---|---|---|
| Chinese | | | | | |
| English | ox | star | water | man | road |

Once people get used to writing, they tend to write faster and faster. The Sumerians, writing about 5000 years ago, found that they could speed up their writing if they gave up trying to draw in the wet clay. Instead, they used a wedge-shaped stick and pressed it into the clay. This changed the way the pictograms looked.

*Development of cuneiform from pictogram*

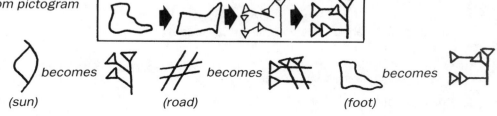

(ox) *becomes*  (sun) *becomes*  (road) *becomes*  (foot) *becomes*

The newer shapes are much harder to read if you don't know the meaning already. This kind of writing is called cuneiform, which means wedge-shaped form. As the Sumerians wrote faster and got more used to recognizing the shapes, they simplified the pictures even more.

Early Chinese writing was carved in metal or wood. It looked like this:

water          mountain          sky

Then Chinese writing came to be done with a brush. That really changed the look of the characters. Brush writing looks like this:

水　山　天

Sometimes we use pictures instead of words to convey messages. International Symbols are used at airports and train stations. They help travellers, no matter what language they speak, find their way around. Can you guess what the seven International Symbols in the picture below mean? Answers on page 96.

Pictures are also used on maps, where writing might not fit. Can you guess at the meaning of these map symbols?

Did you guess schoolhouse, hospital, church, railway track, camp ground, barbed wire fence and bridge?

Pictures are fine for representing objects such as telephones or railway tracks. But some words are not so easy to draw. How do you draw a picture of a "day" or an "argument?" What does "around" look like? Early writers solved this problem by coming up with special pictures to represent ideas. These are called ideograms.

Sometimes people used one drawing to stand for several different ideas. For the Sumerians, "day" was the same sign as "sun." You could tell which was meant by reading the rest of the sentence. In Egyptian, "to go around" was written as a circle. In Chinese, the sign for harmony was made by using a sign for woman plus a sign for house: woman + house = harmony. An especially nice Chinese combination is a picture of moonlight on a window, which means "bright." Can you come up with ideograms for these words: good, danger, luck, scary?

## Sound It Out

Some words seem almost impossible to draw as pictures. For instance, can you draw the word "believe"? You could make an abstract sign like this, ∿ , and teach everyone that the drawing means believe. That's what Chinese writing would do. Or you could make a picture of the sound of believe.

Believe is actually made of two sounds, or syllables: "be" and "lieve." Are there pictures that you could make for these two sounds? What about:

A picture that stands for a sound is called a phonogram. Let's say you wanted to write the word "begun." You could use the same phonogram from your rebus of "believe," ![bee] and add ![gun] (gun) to it. In fact every time you needed a "be" sound you could use ![bee] . When you make a picture for each sound in your language and repeat it, every time you use that sound, you've made what's called a syllabary. A syllabary uses pictures to represent all the sounds in a language. Because there are not as many sounds in a language as there are words or ideas, a syllabary can use fewer pictures than writing made up of pictograms and ideograms. For instance, writing the news in a Chinese newspaper requires at least 7000 different signs. But a syllabary that was developed for the Cree Indians uses about 50 signs. Their spoken language is just as complicated as that of the Chinese, but their written language is much simpler.

### Rebus Puzzles

Using pictures of objects (a bee, a leaf) to make the sounds in a word (believe) is called a rebus. Rebus puzzles are fun to invent and to decipher. Can you figure out these two rebus words? Answers on page 96.

Now see if you can invent some rebus words yourself. Maybe you could try and write a whole letter using only pictograms, ideograms and rebus words. Then see if there is anyone in your family who is clever enough to figure it out.

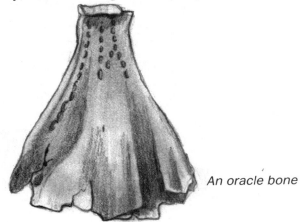

# CHINESE PICTURE WRITING

It's not too hard to learn our alphabet. There are only 26 letters, and once you know them you can write any words you want to—even words that haven't been invented yet. But an alphabet isn't the only way to write. The Chinese use a series of pictograms and ideograms. Their 4000-year-old system is the oldest non-alphabetic system still being used today.

In Chinese, every word or idea has its own picture or group of pictures called a character. Our alphabet, on the other hand, uses the same 26 squiggles over and over again. The following sentence is called an alphabet sentence, or pangram.

*The quick brown fox jumps over the lazy dog.*

That sentence uses all 26 letters of our alphabet. The same sentence in Chinese would look like this:

機伶的棕色狐狸一跳跳過大懶狗。

This is also a pangram:

*He jokingly removed porcupine quills from the zebra's back with wax.*

It uses no new letters, just the same 26 letters as in the "quick brown fox" pangram. But to write the sentence in Chinese you need entirely new pictures:

他開玩笑地用蠟在斑馬背上拔掉箭豬刺。

You have to learn a lot of pictures to read Chinese. Children in Chinese schools use between 600 and 1000 characters (picture signs). There are many more characters that are not used as often—special words that you wouldn't need in school but would for business, farming or law. In all, there are about 8000 characters in use in China today. At one time, there were more than 40 000!

It is thought that Chinese writing developed through the use of oracle bones. Animal bones or shells were pressed with a hot metal tool until cracks appeared. These cracks were "read" and were used to give advice or answer questions. The shapes of the cracks might have influenced the way that picture writing looks. Another idea about why Chinese writing looks the way it does comes

*An oracle bone*

from a legend of a man named Ts'ang-Chieh, who may have lived 5000 years ago. He is said to have studied the marks made by birds' claws, by animal footprints on the ground and by the shapes of shadows cast by trees. He carved these shapes onto sticks and these carvings might have begun picture writing in China.

# CHINESE BRUSH WRITING

Brush writing is highly valued in China. The greatest rulers were also good poets and brush writers. The Chinese make their brushes out of animal hair—everything from sheep hair for a large brush to rabbit hair for a small one. Deer, fox, wolf, mouse hair and even mouse whiskers are used for making brushes. The tools of brush, paper, ink and ink stone are called The Four Treasures of the Room of Literature or *Wên-Fang-Szu-Pao*. In school, children are taught to take good care of these treasures and to respect any writing that is done. Paper that is written on is never torn up. If it cannot be used again and is of no further use, it is collected and brought to a pagoda (a special Chinese house) that is used only for burning paper with writing on it. This pagoda is called The Pagoda of Compassionating the Characters. Writing is treated as if it has a life of its own.

Brush writing is wonderful fun because you can make the pictures look different depending on your mood or on what you are trying to say. You can play with pictures to add to their message.

You can buy special writing kits in some Chinese stores. These kits contain a brush, ink stick, ink stone and paper. An ink stone is used to grind the ink stick on. You put a couple of drops of water onto the stone, rub the stick in it and gradually the ink dissolves from the stick onto the stone. But you don't have to have special Chinese tools to do brush writing. For starters, an ordinary pointed brush and liquid ink or paint will work fine.

1. Hold the brush straight up and down like this:

The fingers should hold the brush firmly and your palm should form a hollow cup.

2. Use only the tip of your brush for writing. Thick lines are made by pressing down, thin lines are made using only the very tip. There are six basic strokes for beginners:

*Horizontal—like a cloud forming a thunderhead*

*Dot—like a rock falling from a cliff with great force*

*Sweeping left—like a rhinoceros horn or sharp sword*

*Vertical—like a thousand-year-old vine stem, strong and stout*

*Sweeping right—like a wave rolling up suddenly*

*Hook—like an eagle's beak*

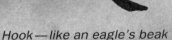

3. Wet your brush with paint or ink (the paint should be fairly thick, not runny) and try these six basic shapes. Then try some of the Chinese characters shown. Look carefully at how each stroke begins and ends.

## Skip the Pictures, Draw Me a Sound

Our alphabet developed gradually over thousands of years. Most civilizations start with pictograms, then go on to ideograms and phonograms to come up with their written language. But some cultures have been able to skip the pictograms and ideograms and go straight to a syllabary. This happens when someone who knows about the idea of writing comes along and meets a group of people who don't have a written language.

A syllabary was invented in 1841 for the Cree Indians of North America by James Evans. The Cree writing system that he invented to do this used fewer than 50 signs, so it was very easy to learn. The Cree people were thrilled to be able to read and write in their own language, and the knowledge of writing spread very quickly. In one small town everyone learned the art of reading and writing in one day! The Cree syllabary that John Evans invented looks like this:

| | | |
|---|---|---|
| LσC | = ma-nē-tō | = spirit |
| σ∧ | = nē-pē | = water |
| σ∧ᵖ | = nē-pa-n | = summer |
| ९ᴛV` | = kā-nā-pā-k | = a snake |

## Where Did Our Letters Come From?

About 4000 years ago, in the Middle East, there were many different groups of people living quite close to each other but speaking different languages. They used to trade food and clothing and other supplies back and forth. One of these groups, the Canaanites, saw that another group, the Sumerians, used little wedge-shaped sticks to make pictures in the clay. These pictures stood for words and sounds in the Sumerian language. The Canaanites thought this was a great idea, so they used the Sumerian pictures for sounds in their language. Of course the sounds in their language had different meanings from the sounds in Sumerian, but it didn't really matter. The pictures didn't have to look like anything in particular — they were just abstract shapes. Pretty soon lots of different groups were using these shapes to show the sounds in their languages.

Try an experiment. Write the letter A on a piece of paper. Then get friends and family to write As on the paper too. Do all the As look the same? Or are there differences? Some people tend to write quickly, some write slowly. Each writer adds a distinctive look to the letter. Over thousands of years, as letters are written by hundreds of thousands of people, they can really change a lot.

The letters that you use today don't look like pictures any more, but they were developed from pictures used by writers who lived in the Middle East, thousands of years ago. For example, we get the shape of the letter A from the Phoenicians, a group of people who lived in the Middle East about 3000 years ago. The Phoenicians had a letter shape called aleph. When letters were pictures, aleph meant ox. It was drawn like a picture of an oxhead: ⋉ (Put some eyes on it and you'll see. It originally looked more like ⟆ if that helps.) The Phoenicians were great sailors and traders. When they started trading with the Greek people, the Greeks liked the look of the Phoenician letter shapes. So the Greeks borrowed them for their language, turning them around a bit. ⋉ in Phoenician became ⟁ or ⟁ and finally A in Greek. This Greek letter is called alpha (from the Phoenician aleph) which in Greek means the beginning — the beginning of the alphabet.

Can you match the Phoenician signs on the left with what they became in the Greek alphabet on the right? Answers on page 96.

| Phoenician | Greek |
|---|---|
| 1. ⅄ | a. θ |
| 2. ⤵ | b. ☰ |
| 3. ⱻ | c. Σ |
| 4. ⊗ | d. K |
| 5. W | e. N |

The Phoenicians used a sign ▽, called beth for house (originally it looked more like ⌐, which was like an open house). The Greeks played with that and came up with ⌀, which turned into β, the Greek letter beta, the second letter in the alphabet.

The Greeks picked up many Phoenician signs and changed them around. By looking at some early Phoenician letters' shapes, you can see how our alphabet (our ox-house) came from pictures.

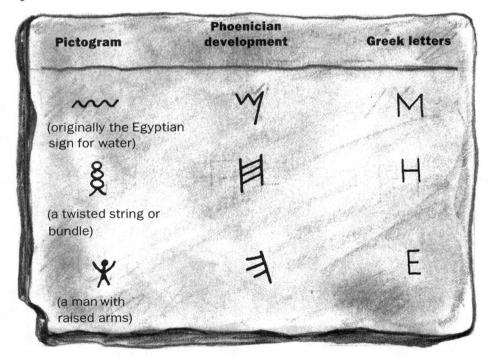

| Pictogram | Phoenician development | Greek letters |
|---|---|---|
| 〰 (originally the Egyptian sign for water) | ⱴ | M |
| ⦵ (a twisted string or bundle) | ⊞ | H |
| ⚉ (a man with raised arms) | ⱻ | E |

When the Greeks finished changing the alphabet, it looked like this:

ΑΒΓΔΕΖ ΗΘΙΚΛΜΝΞ ΟΠΡΣΤΥΧΦΨΩ

Pretty close to what we use today, isn't it?

Eventually, the Greeks were conquered by the Romans. The Romans changed the alphabet to suit the sounds in their language, called Latin. Their alphabet looked like this:

ABCDEFGHIKLMNOPQRSTVXYZ

The Romans took over everybody. They had lots of wars and conquered lots of people. And they taught everybody their new alphabet. They carved it in stone on buildings, archways, stairways, statues and signs. People have been copying them ever since.

Did you notice that the Roman alphabet has only 23 letters? Which three are missing?

These 23 letters were the ones carved on huge stone monuments. They were on display everywhere and people got to know them really well. But when they were written down on smaller surfaces, their shapes began to change. V was often written as U, but both shapes stood for the same short U sound (as in "duck"). Two Vs were put together (VV) to make a long U sound (as in "rule"). Eventually the two Vs (VV) came to be written as W, and V became the sound we know today.

The letter "I" was also used for two sounds, a breathy vowel sound (as in "limp") and a harder consonant sound (as in "jut"). I was changed a little for the consonant sound and became J.

With U, W and J added to the alphabet, there seemed to be just the right number of letters to represent the sounds in many languages. These 26 letters are used throughout the world today.

# THIS ISN'T THE ONLY ALPHABET

Alphabets come in all different shapes and sizes. The world's longest alphabet, the Cambodian, has 74 letters. The world's shortest alphabet is one from the Easter Islands. It is called Rotokas and has only 11 letters.

Here are some letters from the Russian alphabet, called Cyrillic. It was adapted from the ancient Greek alphabet by the Russian people about 1500 years ago.

The letters below are from the Arabic alphabet. They were adapted from the Aramaic alphabet about 1500 years ago. (Aramaic was an early Hebrew language.) Both Aramaic and Greek were adapted from the Phoenician alphabet more than 3000 years ago.

# HOW DO YOU WRITE?

Writing systems are based on pictures, on groups of sounds, or on single sounds (alphabets). Can you guess which of these Hellos comes from picture writing? Answer on page 96.

*Hebrew*     *Cree*     *Chinese*     *Roman (Italian)*     *Devanagari (Hindi)*     *Greek*

# CARVE SOME SOAPY LETTERS

The Romans were experts at carving letters. First they painted their letters on marble, using a wide, flat brush. Then they carved the shapes that the brush made. Even though their letters were carved 2000 years ago, they are still clearly visible today. You can carve letters in soap using almost the same method. Your letters may not last 2000 years but because they're carved in soap, they'll be useful every day!

**You'll need:**
a pencil
paper
a large, smooth bar of soap
a utility or pen knife

1. Draw a friend's initial onto a piece of paper. It should be just slightly smaller than the bar of soap.

2. Place the paper on the bar of soap. If the soap has something already imprinted on it, try to cover it with your letter. Lightly trace around the edge of the letter with a pencil. Because the soap is soft, the pencil will make an impression on it through the paper.

3. Ask an adult to help you make a cut about 5 mm (¼ inch) deep down the center of each part of your letter. Stop before you get to the edge.

4. Make diagonal cuts at the corners of the letter.

5. Cut from the center cut line to the edge of the letter. Do this along all of the edges. These cuts are called V cuts because the cuts make a V-shaped trench in the soap. Long ago, the Romans used this cut when they worked in stone to make their letters clear and easy to read from a distance. Because your letters are in soap, they probably won't last 2000 years, but if you've made deep V cuts, they should last through a few hand washings at least.

PICK up a nice fat crayon and write your name. Now write your name with a ballpoint pen. Do both names look the same? Are they the same shapes and sizes? How did the different writing tools change your letters? The tool you write with affects the way your writing looks. A message written with a stick in the sand looks very different from one carved in stone.

If you didn't have crayons, ballpoints, pencils or markers, what would you write with? Throughout the years, people have discovered many things to make marks with. Sticks were always handy. Sharpen the end and—presto—you have a writing tool. People used pointed sticks to draw messages in wet clay. Dipped in paint or ink, they could also be used to write on smooth surfaces such as stone.

Try using a knife to sharpen a plain stick. (Ask an adult to help you.) Collect some nice flat rocks and some liquid paint and experiment with writing on the rocks. Try cutting your stick in different ways for different effects.

Did you have problems getting the paint onto the stone? You probably couldn't write much without running out of paint. It would take a long time to write this way. The Egyptians had the same problem. So they invented the pen. The Egyptian pen was made from a reed — like your stick, only hollow in the middle. It was allowed to harden and a slit was cut into the end. The slit helped to hold the paint or ink on the reed so that it didn't run out of paint as quickly.

Thousands of years later in England and Europe, people made the same kind of pen as the Egyptians'. There they used feathers or "quills" from birds instead of reeds. In fact, the word pen comes from a Latin word —*penna*—which means feather. Different bird feathers made different sizes of pens: swan feathers made large pens, crow feathers made small pens. Most people used goose or turkey feathers. They were cheap to get because lots of turkeys and geese were raised for food. The quills were softer than reeds but firmer than the animal hair used in brushes. People were very particular about their quill pens — the left wing feathers were best for a right-handed person, the right wing feathers for a leftie. Even today, many calligraphers (people who specialize in beautiful writing) write with quills.

# CUT A QUILL PEN

Until about 100 years ago, anyone who wanted to write needed to be able to cut her own quill pen. Learning to cut your pen was one of the first lessons you had in school.

**You'll need:**
- a utility knife
- a large feather
- a cutting board

1. Ask an adult to help you make cuts to the end of your feather as shown.

2. Cut a small slit in the end as shown.

3. A quill is easier to use if you cut the end at a slight angle. The angle that you cut it at changes depending on whether you are right- or left-handed. Trim the end so that it is comfortable for you to write with.

*Right-handed*          *Left-handed*

4. To write with your quill, dip it in ink, then wipe it off on the sides of your ink bottle so that very little ink is left on the quill. Press very lightly. It may take some practice to get the hang of it. You'll find that you have to dip your quill in the ink quite often—about every other letter or so. You'll soon get used to writing slowly as the scribes did long ago.

*abc*

### Sharpen Your Pen

*Have you ever wondered about the word "pen-knife?" It sounds like a knife you can write with but it's not. Long ago every scribe had to have a pen-knife because as he wrote, his reed or quill pen would get dull and need to be sharpened. The pen-knife was a special knife for cutting pens. As more people started writing, and as more and more writing had to be done, the constant dipping and clipping and dipping of pens was frustratingly slow. Metal nibs that fit into a feather holder were invented. The good news was that these didn't need sharpening. The bad news was that they couldn't be cut to an exact size. Instead, nibs were made in a variety of sizes, and writers picked the size they wanted. When the nib wore out, it was thrown out. Metal nibs were one of the very first disposable products ever manufactured.*

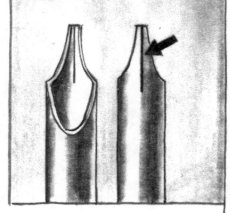

About 100 years ago companies in England and America began to make pens that didn't have to be dipped in ink. The invention of fountain pens meant that the ink could be carried inside the pen.

Fountain pens have a reservoir or barrel in the stem that holds ink.

Ballpoint pens were also invented about 100 years ago by a Hungarian man named Lazlo Biro.

Soft tip or felt pens started to be made in the 1960s. The ink in these pens flows into a soft material, sort of like a miniature sponge. You make a mark by pressing down on this ink-soaked sponge.

A ballpoint is just what it sounds like. A tiny metal ball sits in the end of the pen, in a bath of special quick-drying ink. As you press down and move it around, the ball rolls and spreads the ink on the page. Like a fountain pen, a ballpoint carries its own ink supply with it. Because the ink is thick and a bit oily, it (usually) dries without smearing.

Long ago every scribe or artist made his own ink. Some inks were made from ground-up cuttlefish and molluscs (shellfish) or from dried roots of certain plants. Semi-precious stones like lapis lazuli and malachite were used to make blue and green inks. Even real gold and silver were ground up to make special inks.

The Egyptians and Chinese made black ink from lampblack, the fine black soot that is created when you burn wood or oil. Soot was collected and mixed with water and plant gum or honey. This mixture was then dried into stick or tablet form, to be mixed with water as needed. You can make a soot ink just like the kind used by ancient writers 4000 years ago. Simply put a small piece of charred wood or a piece of barbecue charcoal between several sheets of newspaper. Pound it to a fine powder with a hammer. Mix a large spoonful of the black powder with about a third of a spoonful of honey. Stir it up thoroughly. When you want to write with it, add a few drops of water until it is the consistency you want.

# MAKE CHALK

If you want your writing to be permanent, use a pen. If not, try chalk. It's *really* erasable.

The kind of chalk used in schools is made from a mineral called calcium sulfate, which comes from a substance called gypsum. This chalk recipe uses plaster of Paris, which comes from gypsum too.

**You'll need:**
  30 mL (2 tbsp.) plaster of Paris
  30 mL (2 tbsp.) water
  a piece of waxed paper 50 cm (18 inches)
    long

1. Mix the plaster of Paris and water until they are the consistency of sour cream.
2. Fold the waxed paper in half lengthwise.

3. Pour the liquid plaster in a narrow line down the center fold. Roll the paper around the liquid plaster to form a cylinder, making a mold for the plaster. In about 20 minutes it will set. Don't worry if it feels warm as it sets.

4. Unwrap the waxed paper after half an hour. Let your chalk dry for three days before you try to write with it.

# WHO DUNNIT?

Ink is different from one ballpoint pen to the next. Because of this, you can test and identify which pen was used on a particular piece of paper. This test can be helpful for tracking down criminals—or friends.

**You'll need:**
    6 different black ballpoint pens
    newsprint paper
    scissors
    a glass and water

1. Give a friend the pens and ask him or her to choose one and without showing it to you, write on a piece of newsprint.

2. Collect all the pens and test them to see which one your friend wrote with. To do this, cut pieces of newsprint into strips 15 cm (6 inches) long by 2.5 cm (1 inch) wide. Make a crosswise stripe of ink 5 cm (2 inches) from one end of the strip. Mark on each strip which pen you used.

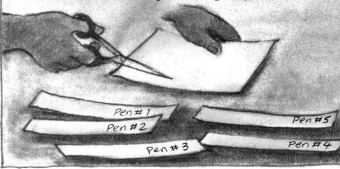

3. Set up a glass that has 2.5 cm (1 inch) of water in it. Place one strip of paper at a time in the water so that the bottom of the strip is in the water but your ink mark is above the water. Fold the top end of the strip over the edge of the glass to hold it in place. The water will creep up the paper and, as it hits the ink, the ink will "explode" in a pattern on the paper. When the ink stops exploding, hang your strip to dry.

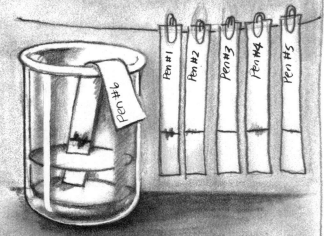

4. After you've tested all the ink samples, run the same experiment on the sample page that your friend wrote on. By comparing the way that the ink on the sample looks with the ink on each of the paper strips, you should be able to determine which pen your friend used.

These days, you can go to the store and buy a rainbow of colored inks made by combining different chemicals. There are special inks that don't clog; inks with plastics and shellacs in them to make their colors glossy and bright; inks that dry fast and spread well through printing machines. But inks have one really big drawback. They don't erase well. If you make a mistake (and everyone does), you're in trouble. Maybe that's why the most popular writing tool is a little hunk of rock that erases really easily—otherwise known as a pencil!

About 600 years ago, some miners in England were digging in the ground, looking for precious gems and minerals. They discovered some soft rocks that were easy to write with. The lines that they made could be easily rubbed off and erased. The idea of a pencil was born.

At first, rough pieces of this rock were used straight from the mine. But it was messy stuff so people had to figure out ways to hold it yet keep their hands clean. Sometimes they wrapped a chunk of it in sheepskin, paper or string. A little piece could be slid into a piece of straw and bound with string to keep it in place. Then the string and straw were peeled away as the rock wore down. Vine twigs were also used to wrap the rock—in fact in some places in England pencils are still called vine.

*Wadd, covered in twine*

The rock, which people at first thought was lead, was called many names including wadd, black lead, kellow and plumbago. It was actually a kind of carbon (the same stuff that turns into diamonds) and was given a new name, graphite, which comes from the Greek word *graphêin* meaning to write. But we still tend to call the black stuff in a pencil "lead."

Pencil leads can be hard or soft. Clay is mixed with the graphite to hold it together, and the amount of clay determines the hardness of the pencil lead. Lots of clay will give a soft line. Less clay will give a sharp line. Pencils are coded with numbers and letters to show how hard the lead is and what kind of line they will produce. B is soft, F is hard, HB is medium, 1 is the softest and 4 is the hardest.

Have you ever wondered how they get the lead inside a pencil?

Pencil makers start with a flat piece of cedar as wide as six pencils.

Six grooves are carved in the wood.

Thin pieces of graphite are placed in the grooves.

An identical piece of cedar is fitted over the first and the two are glued together.

High-speed cutters shape, cut and divide the pencils.

About 100 years ago, someone got the bright idea of putting an eraser on the end of a pencil, making it the perfect writing tool. Although they aren't fancy, wooden pencils are the world's favorite writing tool. People buy and use more wooden pencils than ballpoints, felt tips, fountain pens, metal nib pens, quills, reed pens or Chinese paint brushes. More than 14 billion new pencils are bought world-wide every year. And since most people buy a new one before finishing up the old, imagine how many pencil stubs there are floating around!

## Machine Writing

Some people find scribbling things out by hand too slow. They prefer to use an "Artificial Machine or Method for the Impressing of Letters Singly or Progressively one after another, as in Writing, whereby all Writing whatever may be Engrossed in Paper or Parchment so Neat and Exact as not to be distinguished from Print." That's what Henry Mill called the first typewriter when he invented it in 1714.

Although typewriters have changed a lot since then, the idea remains the same — letter keys are pushed and a metal letter punches an ink ribbon onto a piece of paper. Ink in the shape of the letter is left on the paper. A good typist can type faster than a person can write by hand. Best of all, the letters won't look rushed or sloppy. While everyone's handwriting looks different, a typewriter makes everyone's letters look the same.

A computer works very differently from a typewriter. If you type a letter key on a computer, it makes electrical information appear on your computer screen in the shape of a letter. Having the letter on the screen and in the memory of the computer is different from having the letter on a piece of paper. The only

*An early typewriter*

### MAKE LETTERS YOUR COMPUTER CAN READ

Get a magnifying glass and look at the letters on a computer print-out. Then take a look through the magnifying glass at the letters in this book. Can you see any difference? When people design letters for computer printers to use, they have to remember the dot/no dot language that the computer reads. By coloring in squares on a piece of graph paper, you can get an idea of how letters have to change for the computer.

**You'll need:**
    a pen or pencil
    graph paper

Color in squares on a piece of graph paper to make letter shapes. On a much smaller scale, this is what the computer is telling the printer to do. How much or how little information do you need to give your graph paper printer to get a letter that a

person can read? Here are some examples to get you started:

**NO2**

Try looking at the letters through the wrong end of a telescope or binoculars so that you can see what they would look like small. Are there gaps or holes or bumps in the wrong places? Which of the examples above has a gap that could be filled? Remember, you have to fill in the whole square every time. The computer doesn't understand halves.

way that a computer can print the letter is to turn it into a series of dots and no dots that a computer printer can read. The dots are very small, so small that you don't usually notice them. A good printer can print 1000 lines of dots in an inch!

This dot/no dot language can be sent over telephone lines so that one computer can speak to another. A facsimile (fax) machine takes electronic writing one step further. A fax machine translates a written message or picture into dot/no dot language and sends it over the telephone lines to another fax machine. There it is decoded into words and pictures again. With a fax machine, written words can travel across the world in a few seconds. It's a long way from sticks in the sand.

# WEIRD WRITING STUFF

It's fun to get away from pens and pencils and try some unusual writing tools. Here are some ideas—see if you can invent others. Give yourself big pieces of paper, lots of ink or paint and lots of room. Start by playing around with the letters in your name. Then try making all sorts of patterns with letters made from these tools.

## Tongue depressors

Next time you are at the doctor's, ask if you can have a couple of tongue depressors. Ask an adult to help you cut the end off one tongue depressor. Make the cut at an angle as shown. Stick the cut end into ink or thin paint. Write with it flat on the page, making thick, bold strokes when pulling downwards and thin strokes when pulling sideways. You'll find if you just pull (rather than push) you can make wonderful, large, sweeping shapes.

## Celery

You can write some great letters using the thick end of a piece of celery. Cut it on an angle as you did with the tongue depressor. It's more flexible than the wood and can be made to curve around into different shapes.

## Food

A lot of food comes in circle shapes and straight lines—perfect for letter making. Try an "Eat Your Name" lunch. Cover a plate with soft cream cheese. Then spell out your name with bananas cut into round circles, thin carrot sticks, cucumbers cut into circles, straight and curved pretzels, and any other food you like. The cream cheese will hold your letters in place. Decorate the edges with raisins and parsley to make your name stand out. Then EAT YOUR NAME!

## Jar lids, cardboard and wooden blocks

All letters are made from round shapes and straight lines. Try dipping a round jar lid into your ink or paint to make your circle shapes. Next try using the edge of a piece of cardboard to make the straight lines. What letters can't you make with this method? Can you use only part of your lid to make part of a circle? Or can you bend your cardboard slightly to make other shapes? You can also use a wooden block to make letters, either by "printing" from the edge to make thick straight lines or by pulling the paint-soaked end of the block across the paper in the shapes you want.

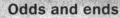

## Odds and ends

What about the feather end of your quill pen? Or a strip cut from a plastic yogurt container? What kind of letters can you make with the end of a peanut shell? Of course the most fun is using your fingers. When you were in kindergarten, you probably did a lot of finger painting. But finger writing, especially if your "ink" is something edible, is even more fun. Cover a plate with chocolate pudding. With clean fingers, try writing your name so that the plate shows through. It may not last as long as writing your name in clay, or even in sand, but it sure tastes great when you lick your pen!

## Write on It

What you write on depends on what's available, how long you want your writing to last and what you're going to do with what you've written. Sand is wonderful stuff to write in but your message may get blown away by the next wind storm. Clay is a bit better because it can be dried and preserved but it still breaks if you drop it. Stone lasts longer than anything. If you really want your message to last, carve it in stone.

About a thousand years ago, Algonquian-speaking Indians carved more than 900 pictures into rock cliffs near Peterborough, Ontario. Cliff carvings are called petroglyphs. The Indians wanted the stories that they carved to be read and remembered for all time. Their carvings are still clear and legible.

People today also like to leave permanent messages. When you want the memory of a person to last forever, you carve a gravestone. Check the outside of your school building and you may find a cornerstone that has the year that the building was built carved into it. The name of your school might be chiselled in stone as well. People use the expression "carved in stone" to mean something that can't be changed.

Carving in stone takes a long time and a lot of hard work. Some ancient people tried painting on stone instead but they soon discovered that paint wears off if left outside for long. To solve this problem, pieces of clay were painted on using a glaze (a special paint for clay made from bits of glass). They were then hardened by being fired in a kiln. In Islamic countries, clay tiles are made with sayings from the Koran written on them. These coloured tiles are used to decorate doorways, walls, fountains and paths. They have lasted as long as the Indian petroglyphs.

Once writing is carved in stone or fired onto clay, it can't be erased or moved easily. But sometimes you don't want your writing to last for a long time. You want to be able to erase it easily. Roman children long ago learned how to write on a wax tablet. This was a wooden frame covered with a thin layer of wax. You scratched through the wax to the wooden surface below with a sharp, pointed stick called a stylus. When the tablet was full, it could be erased simply by smoothing out the wax. The tablet and stylus were made as an easy-to-carry kit.

Most writing surfaces are somewhere between everlasting and easily erasable. People have invented wonderful things to write on depending on what was available. The Egyptians invented a kind of paper made from the papyrus plant, which grows all over Egypt. The stem of the plant was cut into thin strips that were laid side by side and layered crosswise. These layered strips were pounded to release a natural glue in the plant. When dry, the strips all stuck together. The only problem was that papyrus, as it was called, didn't fold very well. (Imagine trying to fold a straw placemat.) But papyrus rolled easily, so the Egyptians made rolls, usually about 7 m (21 feet) long, to write on. Papyrus was a smooth and soft writing surface that

made writing portable and cheap. Because of this, there was more and more writing done. The Egyptians made and sold papyrus throughout the world for more than 2000 years. In fact, we get our word paper from the Egyptian word papyrus.

Although papyrus is still made today, it isn't used very often. Sometime in the 2nd century B.C., in Greece, animal skins replaced papyrus. The skins of cows, calves, sheep and goats were washed, cleaned, scraped and specially prepared to make a smooth, pliable writing surface. Skins could be cut, folded and sewn together into a convenient bundle. The result was a book that was much easier to flip through than unrolling a roll. Skins prepared as a writing surface are called vellum or parchment and are still used today when people want to write something very special.

But animal skins and their elaborate preparation are very expensive. That was fine when only a few books were being made. But when printing was invented, hundreds of books could be turned out in just a few days. One of the very first printed books, a Bible, used about 300 animal skins for a single copy. There were a lot of animals in Europe, but at that rate they'd soon be endangered! With the invention of printing, a cheap, pliable, strong writing surface was needed, one that could

withstand the pressure of the printing press and yet be easily folded and sewn into books. The answer arrived from the Chinese, who invented the art of papermaking.

Throughout the centuries, the Chinese used many different things to write on. In the 7th century B.C., they wrote on silk, which they also used to make clothing. Aside from being very beautiful, silk folds down to a very small size so it was perfect for letters and things that needed to be carried around. Old Chinese stories tell about secret love letters written on silk and carried to their destination by fish or wild geese. One poem tells of how, when a fish was caught, cooked and cut for dinner, a silk letter, 30 cm (12 inches) long, was found inside it! Books were written on pieces of silk 120 m (380 feet) long and then rolled on a wooden holder to form a scroll. But silk was very expensive. Strips of bamboo and wood, which were cheaper, were tied together and used for rough drafts — that is, writing that you might want to change or correct. Only the most perfect and finished writing went on silk.

Then, about 2000 years ago, the Chinese began to experiment with making paper. First they tried pounding together old bits of silk and silk worms' cocoons and mixing them with water. When the water was drained out, the leftover mush was dried on a mat. The Chinese also tried cooking vegetable fibers such as tree bark, hemp (rope), rags and old fishing nets into a mush and drying it flat.

## Goodbye Trees

Next time you read a newspaper or open your mailbox only to find it full of flyers, think of this: 3½ trees are cut down every year to supply one household with newspapers and flyers. It takes 30 years or so for a tree to grow, yet your family uses a tree's worth of paper in just a few months! That's why it's so important to try and reduce the amount of paper you use, wherever possible. When you *do* use paper, try to recycle it. Let your used paper go into making new, recycled paper and save a tree.

The secret of making paper spread slowly from China, reaching Europe about 500 years ago. There, paper was made from rags and bits of old clothing. A "rag man" had the job of collecting these. He walked through town calling out, "Bring out your rags! Bring out your rags!"

Today most paper is made from wood fiber found in trees. The wood is broken down by boiling, pounding and beating.

2. The trees are ground into pulp in a pulp mill.

1. Machines cut down the trees.

The resulting mush is called pulp. Pulp is thinned with water and scooped onto a wire screen to form a piece of paper that is then dried. The pulp and paper industry is one of the biggest and most important in the world. Think of all the paper you use in a day. It's because paper can now be made so cheaply that there's so much of it. If it were as precious as silk, we probably wouldn't have so much junk mail!

## Disappearing Paper

Did you know that the paper you use is disintegrating and crumbling right in front of your eyes? Why? A couple of hundred years ago, people started adding a special chemical called alum to paper pulp to help harden the surface of the paper. Unfortunately, alum combines with the water in paper and forms sulfuric acid, a very strong chemical that attacks the fibres that hold the paper together.

Books printed on acid paper are falling apart. Seven out of every ten books in the world will be dust by the year 2000. People are frantically trying to save books. Books are being sprayed with special de-acidifying chemicals. Many books are being photographed and put on microfilm.

*3. The pulp is made into paper in a paper mill.*

*4. The finished paper is shipped where it's needed.*

# MAKE YOUR OWN PAPER

Make your next letter special by writing it on paper you've made yourself.

**You'll need:**
2 wooden frames, the
   same size, small enough
   to fit in the wash basin
   (picture frames minus the
   glass work well)
nylon window screening
a stapler or tacks
scrap paper (anything but
   glossy or photographic
   paper)
a large bowl
a blender
plant and vegetable scraps
   (cooked broccoli, carrots
   or beets; orange peelings;
   leftover bits of lettuce)
a wash basin
food coloring (optional)
small flowers (optional)
tea towels (at least two)
a sponge
an iron
spray starch (optional)

**WARNING: Ask an adult to help you when using the blender and iron.**

1. Cover one frame with window screening and staple or tack it tightly along the sides. This frame is called your mold. The other frame, without the screen, is called the deckle.

2. Remove any staples or plastic tape from the scrap paper. Tear the scrap paper into small pieces the size of a quarter and soak them in hot water for half an hour.

3. After this pulp has soaked, put a handful of it in the blender, along with enough water to make the blender half full. Blend until you no longer see pieces of paper, adding more water if necessary.

4. Add your vegetable scraps. These will add color and texture to your paper. Blend again to break down the leftovers. Pour the pulp into the wash basin.

5. Repeat this process until you have blended all the paper bits. You may want to color your pulp with non-toxic fabric dye or food coloring. Or you can choose to leave it natural—it usually ends up greyish, depending on what vegetables you added. The paper you buy is bleached with chemicals to get it white.

6. Place the deckle on top of the mold as shown. With both hands, dip the deckle and mold into the basin and scoop up some of the pulp. Gently shake the deckle and mold back and forth to get an even layer of pulp on the screen.

7. Let the water drain away, then place flowers or petals on the pulp. (Make sure to leave room for writing!) Lift the deckle off, leaving the newly formed sheet on the mold screen.

8. Lay a tea towel on a table. Carefully flip the screen over onto the cloth, laying it face down so that the paper rests on the cloth. Soak up any excess water from the back of the screen with a sponge. Then gently lift the screen. The paper will remain on the cloth.

9. You can dry the paper quickly by ironing it. Place another tea towel over top of the paper and iron it at a medium setting. Once dry, gently pull on either side of the cloth to stretch it. This helps to loosen the paper from the cloth. Peel off the piece of paper. If your paper seems too thick, add more water to the basin and stir it all up again. Too thin? Drain off some of the water and add more pulp.

10. In order to keep the ink from blurring and spreading when you write on your paper, spray it with spray starch. This will help the ink to stick on the page.

**WARNING: Do not pour left-over pulp down the drain. Strain it through a sieve and throw it in the garbage or freeze it for later use.**

CHAPTER

THREE

Y OUR choice of writing tool, paper and ink affects the way your letters look. Before the printing press was invented, the look of letters used to change a lot, not just because the tools changed, but because the people doing the writing changed.

Monks were among the earliest of writers. A monk might spend his whole life copying out one book, often a Bible. Monks wanted their writing to be beautiful. For them, each letter was holy because it was connected to God. So they took a lot of time with their decorations and letters. These are the letters T and E from a Celtic gospel written in the 8th century.

But it wasn't just the monks who were interested in books. About 1000 years ago in France, there was a king named Charlemagne (Charles the Great) who loved books and libraries even though he couldn't write his own name. Because he was really rich and had lots of money for animal skins (remember — no paper, and vellum *was* expensive), he could afford to have lots of books copied out (remember — no printing press so books had to be written out by hand). The writing in his books looked like this:

# This style is called Carolingian

The writing style was called Carolingian after Charlemagne. Because Charlemagne liked books so much, his friends and the people at court became interested in books too. As more people wanted to own their own books, more books were written to fill the demand. With more and more books, people became more and more interested in reading. Eventually, ordinary people, not just the wealthy, wanted books. They couldn't afford books like Charlemagne's that used a lot of vellum. So the scribes gradually figured out how to cram more words into the same amount of space. That way a book would use fewer pieces of vellum. The scribes also devised letters that were faster to write. These improvements meant that the books would cost less. A couple of hundred years after Charlemagne, writing in books looked like this:

# This style is called Blackletter

This writing style was called Blackletter because the pages looked black with so many letters squashed onto them. These letters may have used less space, but they looked like a bunch of straight lines—like a fence, some people say. It was very hard to distinguish one letter from the next. For instance, can you tell what this word says:

# minimum

Someone invented dots to go over the i's and j's. This helped enormously. See how much easier it is to read the same word using dots:

# minimum

But even with the dots, the cramped letters are difficult to read. Eventually some writers in Italy decided that they liked the look of Charlemagne's letters better. They modified his style to save space. Two different styles started up. Do they look more familiar to you?

# This style is called Humanist

# This style is called Italic

## Illuminated Letters

In the 14th century, scribes in France and Germany started making special Bibles for rich people. These Bibles were decorated with real gold—the richer you were, the more gold you wanted in your personal Bible. The gold was pounded very, very thin—thinner even than tissue paper. This gold leaf, as it is called, was used to decorate special "illuminated" letters, so called because they shone as though they had a light of their own. Those letters still shine as brightly as when they were first done 600 years ago.

Pictures were sometimes painted into an illuminated letter. These could be of a holy scene described in the text or a portrait of the person who was buying the book. Special artists were hired to do these pictures while the scribes went ahead and wrote out the book. Although some books have hundreds of illuminated letters in them, each one is unique and different.

"Humanist" was a writing style that was considered more "human" than Blackletter. "Italic" writing was named by people in England because it came from Italy. Punctuation was invented around this time, too. Periods, commas, exclamation marks and question marks all help readers understand what the writer has written. Reading without punctuation marks would be very difficult for us now that we are very used to those clues that tell us how to read a sentence we might find ourselves totally lost without them but its nothing compared with whatitmusthavebeenlikebeforetheystartedleavingspacesbetweenthewordswhichishowthissentencewouldhavelookedinthe6thcentury.

Thank goodness for all the writing and reading aids that the scribes developed!

Designers figure out what type of lettering will look best in different situations. Should the letters be simple or fancy? Will they be read close up, or from far away? Which of these signs do you think would be easiest to read from a distance?

## Handwriting and You

Before the printing press, books and important pieces of writing were done in a formal "book hand" style—like the Carolingian and Blackletter styles seen on pages 44 and 45. But you wouldn't write out a grocery list in a formal writing style. People have always had an informal writing style that can sometimes become an illegible scrawl. The way that handwriting looks is affected by many things. One thing is the direction in which your hand moves when writing. Chinese writing is in columns from top to bottom. It tends to flow downwards. You can almost see the movement of the pen down the page.

Our alphabet goes from left to right across the page. That's why our handwriting tends to angle to the right. We slant in the direction we are heading. Left-handed people are at a disadvantage writing from left to right because they cannot see what they are writing. Many lefties write with a backhand slant, possibly because it's easier for them to see their own writing if it loops back towards their hand. When lefties write with wet ink, they have a real problem: they tend to smear their writing as they move over it.

Leonardo da Vinci was a leftie. To overcome the difficulties of writing left-handed, he taught himself to be ambidextrous (able to write equally well with either hand). He also learned to write in either direction, forwards or backwards. Try a trick that he could do. Hold a pencil in each hand and, starting in the middle, write your name in both directions at the same time.

Da Vinci came up with another trick to save him time when he was writing. He wrote one line from left to right and then, when he got to the end of the line, simply headed back the other way.

He liked to write this way because his writing was uninterrupted. It flowed from one line to the next without him needing to lift his pen and carry it to the other side of the page.

The Greeks used to do this on some of their carvings in stone. They called it *boustrophedon*, which means "as the ox turns in plowing" because that was the way you'd move down a field. Most people find it quite difficult to write this way, but computer printers and electronic typewriters use this system with ease. See if you can train your hand and eye to do it like da Vinci!

Many peoples have alphabets that move across the page from right to left, maybe because their first scribes were left-handed. Lettering that moves from right to left looks very different from that which moves from left to right. The direction changes the look of the letters. Our writing system, which goes from left to right across the page, uses letters that face right.

If we wrote from right to left, they'd look like this:

Both the Hebraic and Islamic alphabets move from right to left. Can you tell which direction the pen was moving when it made the strokes?

אם אין אבי לי כן לי לי

اقْرَأْ بِاسْمِ رَبِّكَ

The direction in which our letters face has affected the letters' shape. Almost everybody in our society learns how to write the same shapes, in the same way. Why is it then that no two people's handwriting is alike?

No two people's handwriting is the same because no two people are the same. Your personality deeply affects the way that you write. You are unique and so is your handwriting. Who you are, and the changes that you go through, will be reflected in your handwriting.

### Sweet Letters

In Eastern Europe, it used to be a tradition to give Jewish children a "taste" for writing on their very first day of school. On the first day of *heder* (one-room religious instruction), they would learn their alphabet. The teacher would put honey on the slates where the children wrote. They would lick their fingers as they wrote their first letters and so their first "taste" of letters would be "sweet in their mouths."

Think of the many decisions you make when you write. What kind, color and size of paper to use; pen, pencil or marker; how large to write; where to start on the page; where to stop; how much space between words; how much space around the edge of the page. The list could go on and on. Many of these decisions are not conscious decisions; that is, you may not set out to deliberately leave very little space between each line, but the fact that you did shows something about the way your mind and your personality work. This is the idea behind the science of graphology, or handwriting analysis.

As you change and grow, so does your handwriting. Your signature, which is a very important and personal part of your writing, changes noticeably as you age. Here are samples of the author's signature at age ten and at age 36.

# HANDWRITING ANALYSIS

It's difficult to analyse your own handwriting. Instead, get a sample of someone else's handwriting. Ask a friend to give you a page of writing on unlined paper. It shouldn't be something that she's copied out, but it doesn't matter what it says. There are four fairly obvious things you can observe about her writing: how she's filled the page; her pressure; how she joins the letters; and her slant.

---

## 1. Filling the page

*Small margins, lines filling the space:* This person lives life fully, puts a lot into life.

*Large right-hand margin:* This person likes to play it safe, not take chances.

*Large left-hand margin:* This person is a risk taker, adventurer.

*Size of space left between lines:* Shows how the person organizes his or her life. Are the lines crammed together, the letters of one line tangling with another? Maybe the writer tries to do too much and gets tangled up. Or are the lines far apart, leaving lots of, maybe too much, space between them (a person who gets very little done)? Or do the lines seem a good comfortable space apart?

> On Sunday we went to
> the fair. I liked seeing the
> baby Donkey. His name
> was Thunder. We rode on
> lots of rides. When I
> was on the ferris wheel
> it stopped with me up

> Then she told me that
> I wasn't allowed to go.
> I got so mad! I
> mean just because I
> didn't clean up my
> room she thinks that
> I should be punished.
> So I'm going to pack

> I hope that you can co
> over at my house H
> We can eat chips
> ghost stories and st
> midnight. Bring yo
> bag and a pillow.

> I can't come
> Friday because
> am taking a
> class. But may

*Space between words:* This space shows how a person shares his or her world with other people. Does he need to be close to others all the time (words tightly packed) or does she need to keep people at a distance (words far apart)?

## 2. Pressure

Some people press very heavily on the page, practically carving the letters. Other people's writing glides along the page lightly, hardly making an impression. The pressure that a person uses shows the depth of her emotions, how much she feels things and for how long. For instance, a person with light pressure may not be bothered by deep emotions, may change his mind and heart easily, whereas a person who presses heavily may be set in his ways and very definite about anything he does or thinks.

*he'll probably tell you! all*

*It's a beautiful fall day Some of the flowers have died but*

## 3. Joining letters

How people connect letters shows how they deal with information and learning. Look to see if all the letters are connected or if there are gaps left between letters. Logical thinkers tend to connect everything, while someone who leaves gaps or spaces between letters tends to make more intuitive leaps of imagination. Some people write with a combination of written letters and printed letters called Printscript. This shows logical reasoning mixed with invention. Some people only print their letters. People who print all their letters, without joining any, tend to be independent, aloof and isolated.

*Anyway it's your little ones first on the 18th isn't it, so please give her our love if it*

*AT THE OCEAN this brings BOATS ON THE best wishes*

How people join their letters also shows their emotional connection to other people.

*The Garland:* Connects letters in this shape: ᴜᴜ This person is warm, open and inviting.

*people, the existence of these*

*The Arcade:* Connects letters in this shape: ᴍ This person is strong, supportive and protective.

*let you know that*

*The Angle:* Connects letters in this shape: ᴧᴧ This person is firm and strong-willed.

*I'm afraid I don't have time to get together*

*The Thread:* Connects letters in this shape: ∼∼ This person looks at the overview in life, doesn't want to be tied down, tends to do one thing while her mind is elsewhere.

*I'm not going to send it to you.*

## 4. Slant

How people slant their writing shows the energy they put into life, and into their relationships with others.

*Straight up and down (no slant):* This person tends to be logical, self-contained and even. *Your book arrived in the mail today.*

*Slight slant to the right:* A bit more outgoing. *Let me know where to meet*

*More slant to the right:* Gregarious, reaching out to others. *Please come to my party*

*Extreme slant to the right:* Can be pushy, very involved with others. *I've got to you this*

*Back slant:* Reserved, quiet, held back. *Call me you get to*

These are very simplified ways of looking at handwriting to give you an idea of what graphology is all about. If you want to learn more, an excellent and fun book is *Handwriting and Personality* by Ann Mahoney.

# SIMPLE CALLIGRAPHY

*The word "calligraphy" comes from the Greek words* kali, *which means beautiful, and* graphos, *which means writing. A calligrapher is someone who "writes beautifully." Calligraphers use writing to enhance the meaning of words.*

The biggest difference between calligraphy and ordinary writing is that calligraphy uses a broad- or chisel-edge pen instead of a pointed pen. Pointed pens or pencils make every stroke the same width (monoline) like this: M. Calligraphy uses a wide edge so that the strokes vary in width like this: M. Calligraphy kits have a special pen in them that has a wide edge to it. But you can also buy broad-edge pens and markers separately. They are sometimes called lettering markers and their end looks like this:

**You'll need:**
2 pencils
2 rubber bands
graph paper
a colored pencil
a ruler
a broad-edged pen or marker

The best way to understand how to use a broad-edge pen is to work with two pencils. These make big shapes that make your mistakes and successes really easy to see.

1. Have your two pencils good and sharp. Attach them together with the two rubber bands, one at the top, one at the bottom, making sure the points are even.

2. Take a piece of graph paper. Place both points on a horizontal line and draw straight down. You'll get the two pencils making a line about this far apart:

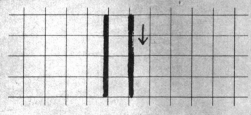

*The arrows show the direction to move your pencils.*

Color in the space between these lines. This shows the width of your widest stroke.

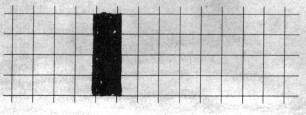

3. Now place both points on a horizontal line and draw sideways. The two pencils should draw over top of each other like this:

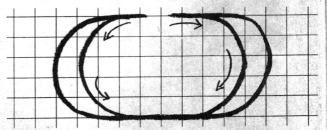

That's your thinnest possible stroke.

4. Now place both pencils on a horizontal line and make a diagonal down to the right. Repeat this to make a diagonal down to the left. The important thing is that, when you finish your diagonal line, the pencils should finish *with both points on a horizontal line.* In other words, your pencils shouldn't twist.

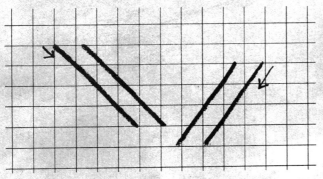

Color these in so you can see them as strokes, rather than lines.

5. Now place both points on a horizontal line and draw a crescent shape to the left, then a crescent shape to the right. Again, they should both end on a horizontal line.

6. What you've just done are the six basic shapes that make up all letters. You've done them with a pen angle of 0°. That is, you held your pencils flat on a horizontal line, and a horizontal line is 0°. If you turn your pencils so that both points rest on a vertical line, you are holding them at 90° to your horizontal. Try doing the six shapes again, this time starting and stopping each time with your points on a vertical line, 90°.

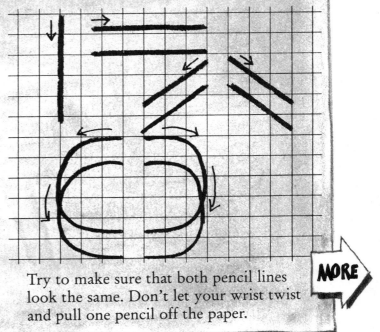

Try to make sure that both pencil lines look the same. Don't let your wrist twist and pull one pencil off the paper.

MORE

7. Now comes the tricky one, but the one that makes it all happen. Take an extra pencil or pen and your ruler. Draw some lines through the corners of the boxes on your graph paper. These lines are at 45° to your horizontal.

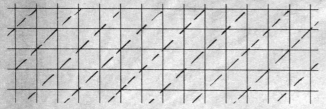

What you need to do now is to draw the same shapes you drew in steps 2 to 6 but start and finish each one with both points on one of your diagonal lines. Don't turn your paper. Draw sets of horizontal lines, about six squares apart. Make your strokes inside these lines as shown. Keep your pencil points held to the diagonal line. You are writing at a 45° pen angle.

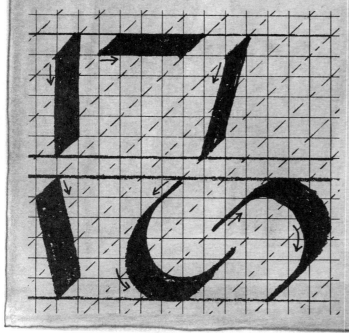

Now you're ready to try doing some letters. Try them first with the double pencils, coloring in the space between your pencils to see your letter shapes.

When you've mastered that, go through the same steps using your broad-edge pen or marker. It's exactly the same idea. Put the whole edge of the marker on your starting line (0°, 90° or 45°) and don't let it twist. All the letters below are done with a 45° pen angle.

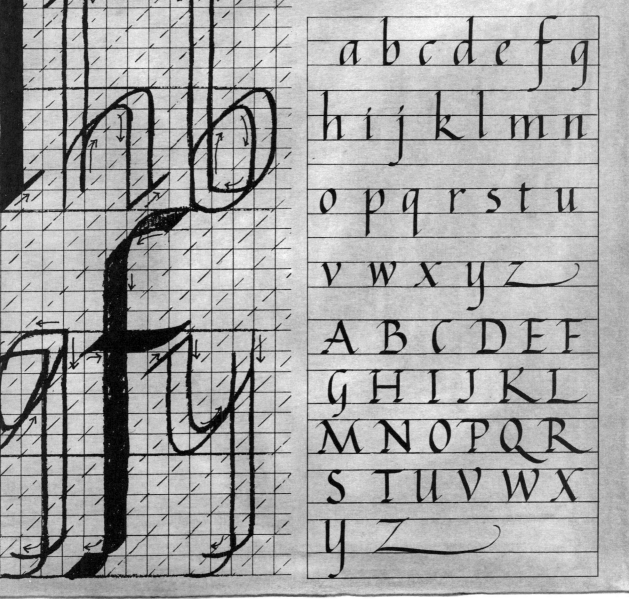

a b c d e f g
h i j k l m n
o p q r s t u
v w x y z
A B C D E F
G H I J K L
M N O P Q R
S T U V W X
Y Z

# CHAPTER FOUR

# Writing & Books

CLOSE this book for a minute and look at the spine. You'll see the title of the book, the name of the author and the name of the publishing house. Publishers turn a writer's manuscript into a book. They bring together the author, editor, designer, illustrator, printer, binder and publicist —all the people required to make a book. There are thousands of publishers throughout the world publishing many millions of books, magazines, journals and newspapers every year.

*The Editor*

Have you ever had a friend or a teacher read a story of yours and say, "It's good, but I don't understand this bit here"? That's what an editor does. It's the editor's job to read an author's manuscript carefully and to make suggestions.

Writers change and rewrite what they've written too, trying to get their writing exactly right. Dennis Lee, who has written ten children's books and many hundreds of poems, says that he has had to rework some four-line poems as many as 30 times. E.B. White, who wrote *Charlotte's Web* and *Stuart Little*, said that a writer should always keep a pair of scissors handy to fit pieces together in a better order. "Do not be afraid to seize whatever you have written and cut it to ribbons; it can always be restored to its original condition in the morning if that course seems best."

A book is usually edited twice. The first time through, editors deal with the structure of the book. They make sure that the focus of the book is right, saying things like "This part is much too long" or "What does this mean?" or "You've already said this (five times!)." The second edit looks for spelling and grammar mistakes and generally helps to polish the writing. This is an example of a page from this book during the second edit phase:

Chapter 2
The Write Stuff

## WRITING WITH MOUSE WHISKERS?

Typeset sentences in order as numbered. Do not set numbers

⑥ Writing your message with a stick in the sand is very different from carving large letters into stone. ⑤ The tool ~~that~~ you ~~choose~~ to write with affects the way ~~that~~ your writing looks. ① Pick up a nice fat crayon and write your name. ② Now write your name with a ball point pen. ③ How did the different tools affect your letters? ④ Are they different sizes or shapes?

If you didn't have crayons, ball points, pencils or markers, what would you write with? Throughout the years people have *discovered many things to make marks with.* ~~written with whatever they could find that~~ ~~would~~ make a mark. ~~The~~ *Sticks were always handy.* ~~handiest thing to grab was~~ usually a stick. ~~You~~ *People used* ~~sharpen~~ the end and -- presto -- *you have* a writing tool. Pointed sticks were used to draw messages in wet clay. ~~Pointed sticks were also~~ *they could also be* dipped in paint or ink, ~~and~~ used to write on smooth surfaces such as stone.

Try using a pen knife to sharpen ~~up~~ a plain stick. Collect some nice flat rocks and some liquid paint and experiment with writing on ~~your~~ *the* rocks. Try cutting your stick in different ways. Did you ~~find that you had~~ *have* problems getting the paint onto *probably couldn't write much without running out of paint.* the stone? You ~~can hardly write~~ a whole letter before having to dip ~~into the paint again.~~ It would take a long time to write this way.

The Egyptians had the same problem. So they invented a pen. The Egyptian pen was made from a reed -- like your stick only *a slit was cut into the end* hollow in the middle. It was *allowed to* ~~hardened and~~ ~~cut with a little slit~~ *so that they didn't* ~~that~~ helped to hold the paint or ink on the reed. *The slit* *run out of paint as quickly.*

## ~~SIDE BAR~~ MAKE A REED PEN

a bamboo stick (buy a small size at a garden supply store)
a saw
a utility knife
a cutting board or hard surface to work on

1. Ask an adult to saw a piece of bamboo 20 cm (8 inches) long.
2. Soak one end of the bamboo stick in water overnight. This is the end you'll cut for your pen. Soaking it helps to soften it for cutting.

*Hundreds of years later in England & Europe people made the same kind of pens as the Egyptians.* ~~had made only~~ *they used feathers, or "quills" from birds. Since they didn't have the same kind of reed flat as the* *In fact the word pen comes from a latin word --*

## The Designer

Open up a couple of books. Do the letters look the same in each one or are they different sizes, shapes? Do the letters fill up the page or are there wide margins (spaces around the edges of the page)? Is the paper white, off-white, or colored; is it thin, shiny or heavy feeling? Is the book a square shape or a rectangle? A vertical rectangle or a horizontal rectangle?

The person who decides what a book should look like is a book designer. A designer wants the book to be easy and enjoyable to read, but also to look right for the subject. For example, you wouldn't want to read an adventure story that looked like your math textbook. The designer decides on the layout of the book—that is, how the letters and pictures, if there are pictures, fit on the page. The designer also decides on the size, the type, the paper and the color of the book.

## The Illustrator

An illustrator draws or paints pictures for a book. These pictures can show parts of a story that the words might not tell. Sometimes pictures are used to explain things that are easier to see than to read about. For this book, the author, the editor and the designer had some ideas about what pictures were needed and where they should be put into the book. The illustrator drew the pictures and the designer decided where they should go on the page.

*The designer chooses the style and size of type to fit the book. Then he or she puts together a rough page layout of the type, leaving spaces for illustrations and showing the margin size.*

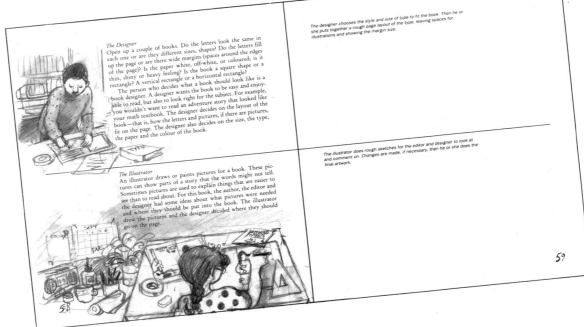

*The illustrator does rough sketches for the editor and designer to look at and comment on. Changes are made, if necessary, then he or she does the final artwork.*

## Assembling the Book

When the author and editor have got the words right, the manuscript is set into type (see page 70). This type is then combined with the illustrations. When everything is assembled properly, it is called the finished artwork. Now it's off to the printer's.

## Printing

A book is not printed one page at a time. As many as 16 pages are grouped together so that they can be printed on one huge sheet of paper. This book didn't use any color inside it so the pages were put through the printing press only once. When color is used, the pages must be printed four times using a different color each time: once for black, once for cyan (blue), once for magenta (red), once for yellow. All of the other colors come from combinations of these four.

*Sixteen pages of a book can be printed on one sheet of paper —eight on one side, eight on the other.*

After printing and folding, the pages must be bound together into a book. Some books are sewn or stapled together. This book is held together with glue that was spread along the back fold of the cover. If you look at the book from the top, you can see glue on the spine.

## Sales and Marketing

Think of the best book you've ever read. How could you get everybody else to read it? How would you let them know about it? What would you say to make them want to read your book? If everybody in your class had a book they wanted everybody else to read, how could you make sure they would read yours? What is special and unique about your book?

Making readers aware of books is the job of the marketing department. Marketing people go to large conventions of booksellers and librarians where they show off their new books. They put ads for books in newspapers and magazines. They arrange for authors to talk about their books in radio and T.V. interviews. Authors also go to bookstores to meet readers and to sign copies of their books. The marketing department thinks up ways to get *you* to ask for the book next time you're in the bookstore or library.

Try your hand at publicizing your favorite book. Think up ways to get people in your school interested in your book. Design posters about the book and ask your teacher if you can put them up around the school. Make bookmarks to give away with the name of the book on them. Would an announcement over the P.A. system help? What other ways can you think of to get your message across? After a week or so of your campaign, check with your friends and see how many have read your book or at least heard of it. Ask the school librarian if people have borrowed the book. See how successful your marketing campaign has been.

# MAKE A BOOK

You can make your own book and be the author, publisher, editor, illustrator, designer, printer and binder all rolled into one. Write a poem, short story, etc., and draw pictures to go with it. Then bind it into a book.

**You'll need:**
   7 pieces of paper 23 cm × 30 cm (9 inches × 12 inches)
   ruler, pencil, pen or marker, eraser
   brown wrapping paper (paper bag) cut to 7 cm × 20 cm (3 inches × 8 inches)
   needle and thread
   waxed paper
   white glue
   2 pieces of cardboard 24 cm × 16.5 cm (9½ inches × 6½ inches)
   plain or patterned paper for cover cut to 26 cm × 35 cm (10½ inches × 14 inches)
   strip of colored paper 26 cm × 7 cm (10½ inches × 3 inches)

1. Put a line down the center of one sheet of paper. This is the gutter (center fold line) of your book.

2. Decide how big you want your margins to be and pencil them in. Draw identical margins on five pages. Remember to use both sides of your paper. The shaded area shown is your writing area.

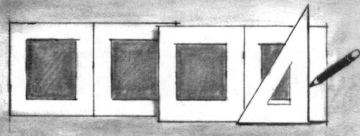

3. Fold these pages along the center line. Put them one on top of the other and write page numbers on each.

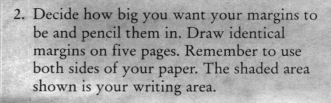

4. You're ready to do a rough layout of your book, deciding where you want the illustrations and text to go. Start your writing on the second right-hand page, leaving the outside page blank. (It will be your title page.) Lightly pencil in the text and illustrations.

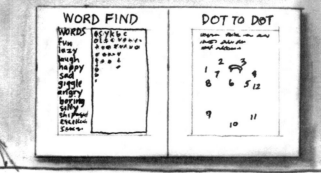

5. Decide on what kind of pen you want to write with and how you want your letters to look (fat, slanted, scary, bouncy). Experiment on an extra piece of paper. Look at other books to get ideas.

endpaper. When your pages are folded one inside the other, the order is endpaper, flyleaf, title page, written pages, flyleaf, endpaper.

BUBBLE

Paint

PRINTING

Computer

markers.

CRAYON

Writing

SHADOW

6. On your title page, also write the author's name (you) and the publisher's name (invent one). Following your rough layout, write in the rest of your book. Draw the pictures in the spaces you left and erase the pencil lines.

7. Now you're ready to bind the book. Take two more pieces of paper and fold them in half to match the rest. One of these will be the flyleaf. It is a page used to protect the title page. The second extra page will become part of your cover. It is called the

flyleaf
endpaper

flyleaf
endpaper

MORE

8. Fold the brown wrapping paper strip in half lengthwise and place it along the fold of your pages. This makes a hinge for your cover. Flatten the book out and sew through all the pages. Sew the gutter

(center fold) from back to front. You may want to use a thimble to help. Knot off your thread at the back when you're finished.

9. With the book closed in front of you, place a piece of waxed paper between the hinge and the endpaper to protect the book as you work with the glue. Apply white glue to the outside of the hinge.

Lay the cardboard on top of the hinge and book. The cardboard should line up with the folded edge. Press down along the hinge area. Leave the waxed paper in place and repeat on the second side. Let the glue dry overnight, then remove the waxed paper.

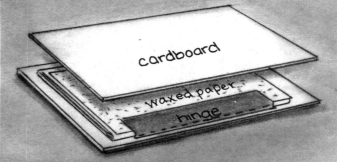

10. Fold the cover paper in half lengthwise.

This paper needs to be larger than the book. Spread glue all along the inside, leaving the center fold area unglued.

Put waxed paper between the endpapers and the flyleaf of your book to protect them. Carefully put the back of the book onto the cover paper with the book open, matching center folds. Fold the excess over the edges as if you were wrapping a present. Press by running your fingers along the folds.

Close the book and smooth the cover paper over the cardboard, pressing out any wrinkles. Let it dry overnight under a pile of books. When the cover is dry, put the strip of colored paper down the spine of the book to strengthen it. Now decorate your cover.

11. Glue your endpapers to the inside of your cover. Make sure your waxed paper is still in place—leave it there until your endpapers are dry.

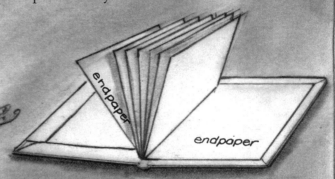

12. Now that your book is all bound and dry, you can make a label or name plate to stick on the front cover. Then stand back and be very proud of your first bound book!

If you want to make copies of your book, get the inside pages photocopied after you've finished your writing and artwork but before you've bound the book. Each copy has to be hand sewn and bound.

## Step Back in Time

Publishing a book is a complicated job, involving many people and many jobs. Long ago, before the invention of the printing press, making books was even *more* time consuming.

The Book of Lindesfarne, a gorgeous Celtic gospel done in the 7th century, took the scribe, Bishop Eadfrith, nine years to complete. And that was just one copy! Each and every word had to be written out by hand. What was needed was a way to make many copies, quickly.

Around 594 A.D., the Chinese invented woodblock printing. Words, pictures and designs were carved into a flat piece of wood. This woodblock was then covered with ink, and paper was pressed and rubbed onto the block so that the ink was transferred. In only a few days, hundreds of copies could be made from the same woodblock. But there were problems with this method. Letters had to be carved backwards onto the wood so that they would print correctly. And it was very difficult to make changes. If you made a mistake or wanted to add something, you had to re-do the whole block. Making an entire book still took a long time, because each page had to be carved separately.

*A woodblock (right) and the printed page (left)*

Around 1450, a man who lived in Germany, named Johann Gensfleisch zum Gutenberg (usually called Johann Gutenberg), figured out a way to solve these problems. He made pieces of type — individual metal letters that could be put together in whatever order they were needed. For instance, if you wanted to print the words "pat" and "tap," you could use the same three letters and just reverse the order. You didn't have to carve out a whole new word for each. This new way to print, using movable type, wasn't all that new. In Korea, around 1200 A.D., books were printed using metal blocks as well as individual metal and wood letters (or characters — the Koreans use a writing system similar to the Chinese). But the idea didn't really catch on and spread until Gutenberg's invention.

To make the pieces of type, Gutenberg would carve a letter in relief on a steel rod. This means that the letter sticks up from the surface of the background.

The carved piece is called the punch. It is punched into a slab of soft brass, leaving an impression. You'll notice that the letter is backwards. It has to be, so that it will print the right way around. This brass impression is called the matrix, or mother. Hot molten lead is then poured into the matrix to make the piece of type. Thousands of "children" type, all looking the same, can be made from the one mother matrix.

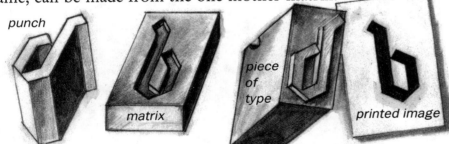

punch · matrix · piece of type · printed image

Carving letters out of metal is very different from drawing them with a quill pen. Some things that a pen can do just don't work on a piece of type. People had to think carefully about the way letters looked, since every single letter was going to be the same. These people were type designers. Like the scribes before them, they made different styles of letters for different purposes. In fact, many of the first type designers were scribes who had been put out of work by the new printing presses.

## Count the As

Each book uses thousands of letters. Take the letter A, for example. How many As can you find on this page? Answer on page 96. To figure out approximately the number of As in the entire book, you multiply the number of As on this page by the number of pages in the book. That's a lot of As! If you were making this book by woodblock prints, you'd have to carve each one of those As. But with type, you need to carve only one A to make as many As as you need. And the As that you make for this book can be re-arranged in a new order for another book.

## Mind Your Ps & Qs

Has anyone ever told you to "mind your Ps and Qs?" This usually means to be careful and pay attention to what you are doing. The expression comes from the early days of printing. Pieces of type were laid out in special cases or drawers (typecases) where there was a compartment for each letter. The letters were laid out alphabetically so that the typesetter could easily find the one he needed. That meant that the letter p came right beside the letter q. In order to print the right way around, the pieces of type had to be made with the letter showing backwards. So p became q and q became p. The typesetter had to be careful and mind which he was using, his p's or his q's.

We also get the terms "upper case" and "lower case" from typesetting. All the capital letters were put into the case on top (UPPER CASE) and all the small letters were put into the case below (lower case).

In order to print a page using movable type pieces, you put all the letters in the correct order, only backwards so that they'll print the right way around. This is called "composing" the page. You can make corrections easily by changing around some of the pieces of type.

Using movable type instead of woodblocks meant changes in the printing method. Gutenberg found he needed something to help him press the paper onto the type. So he took a large screw-press used for squeezing oil out of olives and juice out of grapes and adapted it for his printing machine. Then he found that his old printing inks didn't work and he had to invent a new ink that would stick on the metal type and transfer onto the paper properly.

Gutenberg's inventions spread like crazy. People really wanted books! Schools were especially thrilled — now students could have their own books instead of having to share the same one. Within a few years, every major city in Europe had a printing press. In the 40 years after Gutenberg's invention, more than 40 000 different books were printed and many thousands of copies of each. But it wasn't just books that were affected. A lot of Gutenberg's business was printing calendars and pamphlets. Because of his invention, things could be printed quickly, cheaply and in large quantity. News could suddenly be spread to lots of people while it was still new. Newspapers, and the very idea of *news*, were invented. Gutenberg's invention has often been called the single most important invention for human civilization. Because so many more books, pamphlets and newspapers could be printed, many more could be read. More people learned how to read and so more people wrote. Reading and writing became skills everyone needed, not just the accomplishment of a few learned men. Suddenly ideas could be communicated to a vast number of people. It was the beginning of what is called mass communication.

## Type Designs

New type designs are being created every day. If you look closely at all the printed words around you in books, newspapers, posters, ads, junk mail, you'll start to notice that there are a lot of different looking letters. This is because letters have different parts to them that can be changed to make different lettering styles.

A letter can have parts that are thick, parts that are thin, or have all parts the same width.

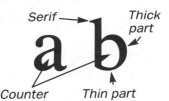

A "serif" is a short stroke beginning the vertical part of a letter. Some letters have them, some don't. Letters that don't have serifs are called sans-serif. A "counter" is the space inside a letter. It can be round, squarish or oval shaped.

Which of these letters have serifs? Which are sans-serif? Answers on page 96.

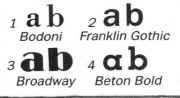

1 **a b** Bodoni

2 **a b** Franklin Gothic

3 **ab** Broadway

4 **αb** Beton Bold

The author writes the manuscript.

The editor edits the manuscript.

The typesetter produces the finished type.

The designer designs the pages by hand or by computer.

The designer puts the type and illustrations on the artboards.

## Manuscript

The word "manuscript" now means a book or an article as it appears before it is published or printed. It is usually typewritten or printed by computer. But the word came into being when the printing press was invented. It came from *manu,* which means hand, and *scriptus,* which means writing. So a manuscript was something that was handwritten, instead of printed.

## Typesetting and Printing Today

When printing was first invented, a person called a compositor picked out the pieces of type one by one and arranged them as needed for each page. Some people still like to print beautiful handmade books in this way, but these days handprinting is considered much too slow. Gutenberg could print up 300 sheets of paper a day, which was considered an amazing number in his day. Today's machinery can print 5000 to 10 000 sheets *per hour.*

The book you are reading right now was typed into a computer, which changed the words into "digitized" information that other computers are able to read. A second computer converted this electronic information into a new visible form, this time in the type style chosen for the book. This type was then laid out and combined with illustrations according to the author's and editor's intentions, and these layouts were then photographed by the printer's camera. All the letters and the lines of the illustrations appeared next in negative form—clear

The artboards are photographed and film is made.

The film is used to make a printing plate.

The plate is wound around a cylinder on the printing press. Ink is applied to the plate and paper is sent through the press.

CAMERA

WATER SOLUTION

PLATE CYLINDER

BLANKET CYLINDER

INK

PAPER

IMPRESSION CYLINDER

lines on a black film background. By means of chemicals and light, the clear images were transferred onto a thin sheet of metal. This metal sheet, called a plate, was then used to print the book by a process called offset printing.

In offset printing, this plate, carrying the pictures of the book's pages, is curved around a large roller and inked. The ink sticks to the places where the letters and pictures are but is washed off the blank parts with water. The roller turns and presses the ink onto another roller called a blanket. This blanket roller turns and presses the ink onto large sheets of paper. In this way, the images of the photographed pages from the metal sheet are transferred onto the paper.

Long ago when books were printed using metal type, pressure was needed to press the ink onto the page. If you ran your finger along a page printed this way, you could feel the impression of the type. But if you run your finger along this page, you can't feel the letters or the ink at all. With offset printing, the ink transfers with no pressure, so gently in fact, that it is called a kiss impression.

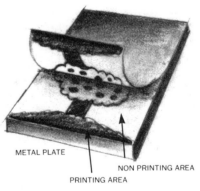

METAL PLATE

NON PRINTING AREA

PRINTING AREA

### The Offset Lithography Printing Process

The non-printing areas are treated so that they absorb water and repel ink. The ink sticks only to the area to be printed.

## How's Your Spelling?

Before printing, spelling used to change, depending on how the word sounded. The same words sound different when said by different people. This is called dialect. When a scribe wrote, he would spell words as they sounded to him. Different scribes would spell words according to the dialect of where they lived. So, for instance, the word "when" was spelled "whan," "wonne," "hwanne" or "qwenne" depending on how it was said. Because scribes wrote so few books, and people read so few, not many people were aware of spelling differences. When printing began, printers picked one spelling and used it for thousands of books. With so many books using "when," people became used to that spelling. As more books were printed and people read more, spelling became standardized.

## Binding It All Up

What would you do if you had a pile of pages to keep together? You could make a special box or folder to put them in called a portfolio. But every time you wanted to read a page, you'd have to rummage through. Pages could easily get mixed up or lost. Imagine trying to read *this* book if all the pages were loose and out of order! Book binding holds the pages together and protects your book.

Probably the earliest form of book binding was with clay. In the 8th century B.C., the Sumerians sometimes put their clay tablets into clay envelopes with the title of the tablet stamped on the front. The Egyptians and Romans wrote on papyrus sheets, which they glued side by side to make one long page. This long page was then rolled up on wooden spools into a long scroll and put in a wooden cylinder to protect it.

Books and laws of the land were written on scrolls for thousands of years. But reading them could be a pain, especially when some were 45 m (148 feet) long! If you wanted to find something mid-way through the book you'd have to unroll and reroll, unroll and reroll. In a long book, it could be difficult to find what you were looking for. A whole book wouldn't fit on a single roll — it sometimes took 20 to 30 rolls for one book. Imagine if all the books in your library were on scrolls — you wouldn't have room for the people!

Around 200 A.D., people started sewing individual pages of papyrus together. Pages could be sewn down the middle and folded into a book instead of glued and rolled. But papyrus doesn't last very long when it is folded. It breaks. By about 400

A.D., people were using vellum and parchment to write on and these folded beautifully. So a whole new way of putting books together was invented.

Pages were piled on top of each other, folded in half and sewn down the middle. The writer had to leave a space down the center of the page with no writing on it, where the fold would happen. This blank middle space, which you can see on the pages of this book, is called the gutter. Writers discovered that if they were making a big book, they couldn't pile all the pages on top of each other, then fold and sew through them all. The pages wouldn't stay folded and it was hard to sew through that many at a time. (Try it yourself: take a pile of 50 pieces of paper and try to fold them in half. Even if you can fold them, you'll find they don't fit together very well.) So pages were sewn together in groups of 8, 16 or 32. These groups are called signatures. Several signatures were sewn together to make a whole book. If you look at the binding of this book from the top, you can see how the pages are folded into groups.

Sewing the pages helped to keep everything together, but the outside pages tended to get damaged and the stitches pulled out. Also, vellum swells and fattens with the weather. People needed a way to protect the pages and keep them held shut. So they put wooden boards on the top and bottom and clasps on the sides to keep the book shut. This way of making a book is called the codex method from the Latin word *caudex*, meaning the bark of a tree. Eventually, the boards and back of the book were covered in leather that was beautifully carved and decorated with gold and jewels.

Keep rolling!

Books today are often held together with staples or glue, and their covers are likely to be cardboard or heavy paper. But the way that they are put together is still called the codex form. It's a really easy way of reading and looking up information—much

# MAKE AN ACCORDION

An accordion-fold book is based on a Chinese way of presenting poetry and artwork. It's half-way between a scroll and a codex. With this kind of book, you can turn the pages to look at them one at a time or you can leave the book partially opened on a table, as a display.

**You'll need:**
 a long, thin sheet of paper
  approximately 9 cm
  (3½ inches) wide ×
  90 cm (36 inches) long
 2 pieces of cardboard
  10 cm × 8.5 cm (4 inches
  × 3¼ inches)
 glue
 fabric ribbon
  1 cm × 45 cm (½ inch
  × 18 inches)
 waxed paper

1. On your long strip of paper, draw a line 7.5 cm (3 inches) from the end and fold along that line.

2. Carefully fold the whole length of paper in valley and hill folds, making sure that the edges match. Now write out your story and illustrate it.

7.5 cm (3 inches)

easier than unrolling scrolls or sorting through loose pages. The invention of codex books 1600 years ago went a long way to making reading a pleasant and enjoyable experience.

# FOLD BOOK

3. Draw lines 5 mm (¼ inch) from each edge of your cardboard.

4. Put glue onto one piece of cardboard, staying inside the lines.

5. Lay the middle of your ribbon down on the centre of the cardboard. Place one end of your folded paper over the ribbon onto the board, inside the lines.

6. Put glue inside the second piece of cardboard, leaving the edge with no glue as you did in step 4. Glue the front end of the paper to this board.

7. Put a piece of waxed paper over the glued page and put a book on top. Repeat for the other end. Let the glue dry completely before taking out the waxed paper and closing the book. You can use the ribbon to hold the book closed, tying it at the front or at the side.

EVERY time you pick up a pencil or pen and make words on a page, you are being a writer. As a writer you make choices, sometimes without even thinking about it. You decide who you are writing for and whether you want to write the truth or something made up. All writers make these choices when they write.

Maybe you write just for yourself. Many people keep diaries or journals that are meant to be read only by themselves. Or you could write for one other person — write a letter. Or you could write for lots of people that you've never met. Books, newspapers and magazines are read by thousands of people whom the writer doesn't know. Chances are that, so far, your writing has been for just a few people to read.

Are you writing about true things or something you've invented? When you write out invitations to your birthday party, you are writing about a true thing. You are writing non-fiction. But when you write to your cousin Sarah about the birthday party you had with 100 kids, 50 ponies, 75 movies, 600 gallons of chocolate ice cream, 828 incredible presents and no grown-ups, you're probably writing fiction, about an invented thing.

This book is a non-fiction book. It is about true things. You read non-fiction when you want to find out some information. People usually write non-fiction because they want to pass on some information about something.

Fiction is different. Fiction is made-up stories. Ever since human beings first started to talk, they have made up stories about their lives and the world around them. There are many different reasons why people write fiction. Some authors write because they feel there is a person or a story inside them that wants to get out. Some writers write to make new things happen that haven't happened yet. Writers use language to play with ideas and to experience things that might never happen in real life.

## Getting Started

Writing a story is like using bits of true things to make up a lie. And like a lie, once you get started it's often quite hard to stop. But getting started can be a problem. Sometimes it's hard to know what you want to write about. C.S. Lewis, who wrote the Narnia stories, said that you should always start with something that you care passionately about. If you're not interested, no one else is going to be.

Sometimes when writers start writing a book, they don't yet know what their book will be about. They often start with an idea, a memory or a bit of overheard conversation. If they can

### Make an Alphabet Book

If you can't think of an idea for a whole story, start with an alphabet book. Decide on a theme, something you're really interested in such as animals, places, food, movies or superheroes. Then make up a sentence with words beginning with the letter for that page. (Batman's beautiful batmobile is all broken and busted up.) You'll be surprised at how many things you'll be able to invent for your alphabet story. Try doing illustrations for each page, too!

## Playing with Words

A builder must know his or her tools, and so must a writer. These two word games will let you play with your tools.

*Non-repeaters*
Try to write a short story that never uses the same word twice. You'll find it takes careful thinking. (Those two sentences are non-repeaters.)

*Ten to one*
Write a short story, in which each word counts. The first sentence of the story should have ten words, the second sentence nine words and so on down to the last sentence, which has only one word. It's tricky, but fun.

get a first sentence, it will often lead them on to the second, and on and on. Look at the first sentences in books that you like. How do they make you want to read on? Here are a few examples to get you going:

"Where are you going with that ax?" (*Charlotte's Web* by E.B. White)

"One thing was certain, that the white kitten had nothing to do with it — it was the black kitten's fault entirely." (*Alice Through the Looking Glass* by Lewis Carroll)

"In twenty minutes I, Maynard Chan, will be on national television." (*Hiccup Champion of the World* by Ken Roberts)

"It began with a game of hide-and-seek, and that would never have happened either if Valerie hadn't lost her temper." (*Space Trap* by Monica Hughes)

Some writers know what they want to write about but have a really hard time getting down to it. Astrid Lindgren, who wrote the Pippi Longstocking books, couldn't make herself sit down to write about Pippi until one winter when she sprained her ankle and was forced to stay in bed. P.L. Travers wasn't able to write *Mary Poppins* until she was recovering from a serious illness. But you don't have to get sick to write. Some writers do research to get them going. They read about or travel to the place where their story is to happen. Or they look carefully at the world around them to get ideas for their stories. Hans Christian Andersen said, ". . . often it seems to me that every fence, every little flower said: 'Just look at me, then you'll know my story,' and if I so desire, the story is mine."

Some writers say that writing is like fishing. They suggest you sit where no one will disturb you, maybe in the quiet of an early morning, and wait for the nibble of a thought or idea. No fish are too small for this pond. Write down ideas as they come along. After you've landed a couple of ideas, let a problem creep in. Before you know it, you're writing!

But once you get going, you still might get stuck. This is called writer's block and writers have many different ways of overcoming it. In the middle of writing a story, writers might have to get up and wash the kitchen floor (even when it's not dirty), sharpen a box of pencils, bath the dog, eat all the food in the refrigerator, walk to the farthest store possible and buy a

piece of gum. But all the time, they're still writing—waiting, as Maurice Sendak says, for their unconscious mind to throw them a word.

Sometimes if you're stuck, it helps to throw some "what ifs" into your story. Asking yourself questions is a good way of finding out what might be happening. After answering the what ifs, you may have some more problems to work on or new characters to introduce. The end of the story will come when the problems are solved. Many writers say that their stories don't always end the way they were expecting. You may end up surprising yourself.

Starting with one small idea, throwing in some problems, some what ifs and some characters—suddenly there's a whole story. Something that didn't exist before now does. But it's important to remember that it was with *words* that the story came alive. Words are the building blocks and with them you can make anything you want. Playing with words is the best way to get to know them really well.

## The Longest Word

Here's a word that was originally written out in ancient Greek:

*lopadotemachoselachogaleokranioleipsanodrimhypotrimmatosilphioparaomelitokatakechymenokichlepikossyphophattoperisteralektryonoptekephalliokigklopeleiolagoiosiraiobaphetraganopterygon.*

It's the longest word ever written and it means a cooked dish of sweet and sour ingredients including mullet (fish), brains, honey, vinegar, pickles, marrow and ouzo (a Greek drink). It's hard to imagine saying that, let alone eating it!

## What Are You Writing?

People write diaries, letters, poems, plays, comic books, newspapers, magazines and books. Which form a writer decides on will depend on the kinds of words she likes to use and on who she wants to read her writing. For instance, private writing (such as a love letter) uses very different language from public writing (such as a newspaper).

### Journals and Diaries

Do you have a diary with a lock on it to prevent other people from reading it? A locked diary makes you feel free to put down your innermost thoughts, doesn't it? Some people find that diary writing helps them to understand their own thoughts and feelings.

Some diaries and journals get published later as books. *The Diary of a Young Girl*, by Anne Frank, was found by friends of Anne and published after she died. Anne and her family lived in hiding during the Second World War. She wrote the diary to help herself, but people throughout the world have read the book and learned a lot about her life and about what it is like for people who are forced to live in hiding.

If you don't have a diary, why not try it? A good way to start is to answer the question "What is the biggest thing that happened to me today?" Write down what you thought and felt about that event. Writing may help you to open up parts of your mind and get at thoughts and memories that are otherwise forgotten. If you start from that simple question, you'll be surprised at how much there is to tell.

### Letters

Letters are a kind of one-sided conversation. Before the invention of the telephone, people used to write great long letters to each other. Travellers and explorers sent letters home describing the new lands they saw.

Sometimes it's easier to write things in a letter than to say them out loud. Have you ever tried to tell someone you're mad or that you love him? Pick up a pencil and write.

Most letters are meant to be read only by the person to

whom they are addressed. The wrong person reading your mail can mean big trouble. Mary, Queen of Scots was a 16th-century queen. She sent secret letters to Lord Bothwell, asking him to help her kill her husband. When these letters were found by a spy, Mary got into a lot of trouble. She was put in a jail in the Tower of London. From the Tower, Mary wrote letters to friends asking them to help her try to escape. This time she wrote the letters in code that looked like this:

b g ɯ m H ɔ f a σ ɟ k σ ɯ x ∞ : ℝ Ⴆ ✝ ⊥ ⊥⊥ ɱ ʃ ᴏ ✝

a b c d e f g h ij k l m n o p q r s t u v w x y z

But the code was pretty easy to figure out. When she wrote a letter about trying to kill the Queen of England, Elizabeth I, and the queen got hold of the letter, Mary's letter-writing days were over. Queen Elizabeth ordered Mary, Queen of Scots beheaded.

σbℝo Ⴆ✝⊥bℝ✝

*mary       stuart*

OFF WITH HER HEAD!

## GET YOURSELF A PEN PAL

When you write to a stranger, you can find yourself looking at your life and seeing things through someone else's eyes. At the same time, reading about someone else's life helps to put your own in perspective.

A pen pal is someone with whom you exchange letters. Very often you don't know your pen pal before you start writing to him or her. But as the letters and the years go by, you may find that your pen pal becomes your best friend!

If you would like help finding a pen pal, write to one of these organizations:

American Sharing
  Program
5473 Commercial S.E.
  #20
Salem, OR
U.S.A. 97306

The Pen Pal Post
559 Pape Ave.,
Toronto, ON
Canada
M4K 3R5

International Friendship
  League
55 Mt. Vernon St.,
Boston, MA
U.S.A. 02108

Correspondence Canada
2695 McWillis Ave.,
Montreal, PQ
Canada
H4R 1M5

## Write a Sense Poem

Try writing a sense poem about your favorite sport. Use words that feel like the way you feel when you do that sport. For example, you could write a poem *about* running that went like this:

I ran up and down
and all around
'round about
'til I tired out.

But all that does is rhyme. It doesn't give you the *feel* of running. A sense poem about running might go like this:

Feet
Up
Down
Push
Stretch
Breathe
Up
Hard
Down
Hard
Huff
Hard
Push
Stretch
Ouch
Up
In
Sweat
Push
Whoosh!

Does this give more of a running feeling? Try it with a sport you know really well. Try to remember what it feels like. Don't worry about trying to make it rhyme.

## Poetry

Sometimes writing is matter of fact and straightforward. Sometimes it is full of images and imaginative sounds and words. Poetry plays with the sound of words. It has a musical feel to it. The words are arranged in a pattern to give the poem rhythm and, sometimes, rhyme. Before the written word was invented, long stories were told in rhyme. Although these epic poems were very, very long, the rhythm and rhyme made them easier to memorize. But even after the invention of writing, people wrote long poems because they still liked to use the sound of words.

## Plays

People who write plays think a lot about the sound of words since their words are meant to be spoken. A playwright has to listen to people carefully to try and capture the sound of the way that people speak. Also, because a play is visual, a playwright can leave things unsaid, letting the stage set and the actors' reactions convey meaning.

## WRITE A DIALOGUE PLAY

A dialogue is a conversation between two people. Some writers write a dialogue to help them prove a point. They invent two characters and let them have an argument so that the reader or listener will hear both sides of the argument. Then the writer will allow one character to win the argument.

You can write a short dialogue play to help you win an argument. Use a very familiar argument—like the one about *cleaning your room*! See if you can remember some of the things that each "side" said. Try to write the dialogue just as it was spoken in real life. Only this time, if you want, *your* character can come out the winner.

Try drawing a *comic strip* of the same argument. You may want to change the language to make it sound more adventurous. You might even want to make the argument between a super-you, capable of saving the world (so who's got time to clean her room!?), and the evil-fanged mother-screecher, the terror of Metropolis, who slams doors, threatens doom and destruction on your dessert and promises to erase your favorite tape!

*You did so!*

*I did not!*

*Newspapers*

Imagine if your writing were read by 62 826 273 people at the same time! That's how many newspapers are delivered or bought *every day* in the United States. In Canada, 4 653 000 copies of various newspapers are printed every day. Now that's getting your message across!

Newspapers are about the news. The news can be local ("Last Friday, Lyla Nault's cat had four baby kittens.") or world-wide ("Last night, an earthquake hit the city of Beijing, China."). Newspapers must be printed quickly and cheaply so that the news can get to people while it is still *new*.

Newspapers came into existence when printing was invented. The oldest continuous newspaper, *The Peking News* (Tsing Pao), came out monthly starting in 600 A.D. when it was printed up using woodblocks. It was published regularly for more than 1300 years, until 1935.

*Magazines*

There are magazines devoted to just about any subject you can think of. For instance, the *Flat Earth News Quarterly* is a magazine dedicated to proving that the earth is flat and that space travel is a hoax. *Kite Lines* is a quarterly magazine of kite plans and kite-flying techniques. These magazines sell between 2000 and 5000 copies every three months. The most popular magazine in the United States, *T.V. Guide*, sells 16 800 441 copies every week!

*Books*

Newspaper reporters know that what they have written will be read that day, or not at all. No one reads yesterday's news. But the author of a book knows that, if the book is good, people will be reading it for years to come. Books last and can wait patiently on the shelf for readers to find them.

Approximately 700 000 new books are published world-wide every year. Some of these books are only read by a few people. Others may be reprinted many times, selling many hundreds of thousands of copies. The Bible is the all-time best-selling book but it's impossible to estimate how many have been sold since it was written 2000 years ago. But in recent times the *Guinness Book of World Records* has sold the most copies of any book. In its 34 years of publication, it has sold 61 million copies in 31 different languages. That's some record!

# MAKE A NEIGHBORHOOD NEWSPAPER

Why not write your own newspaper filled with neighborhood news? Ask your friends to contribute news and ideas. Phone the local weather office to get a prediction on upcoming weather. Try to be fair and honest when you report the news. As more people see your paper, they will get involved and give you more news, ideas and stories.

Most newspapers have several kinds of articles. Yours could, too.

*Features:* what's been happening in the neighborhood

*Editorial:* your opinion, what you think about what's been going on

*Weather:* what it's been, what it's going to be

*Classified:* Lost and Founds, Want Ads (jobs that people need done), For Sale or Rent (things that people want to buy, sell or rent)

*Comics:* invent your own characters

Look through a newspaper to get ideas for some other sections. You might want to include sports news or book reviews. When you've got all of your news written, you can type it or write it out neatly and make photocopies of it to pass around. Don't forget to give your newspaper a good title that people will remember and ask for!

## A Home for Writing and Ideas

How do you find out about things? If you want to know how to raise horses or build a spaceship, you try to find some writing on the subject. People have written about everything imaginable. If you don't have the information that you need, you can go to the place where writing and ideas are kept—the library.

Ever since writing began, people have wanted copies of what was written. When books were handwritten, there weren't many copies available. If a book was lost or ruined, the ideas and thoughts written in it could be lost forever. In ancient Greece, where some very important thinkers lived, people began to gather to talk and exchange ideas. They shared around the few books that they had and wrote out extra copies of them. The idea of a library was born.

Many rulers thought that having their own libraries and museums would show their intelligence. The Egyptian king Ptolomy I started collecting books in the ancient city of Alexandria 2300 years ago. His was the first really big library.

At that time, books were written on papyrus rolls that averaged 7 m (21 feet) in length. It is thought that the library at Alexandria had 250 000 such rolls in it. Finding what you wanted in all those rolls was a nightmare, until someone figured out a way to remember which rolls were where. It was the first library to have a cataloguing system. Unfortunately, the library at Alexandria was burned during a civil war in 200 A.D. Many writings were lost forever—we know about them only through other writers who happen to mention them.

In the 8th century, the French king Charlemagne wanted to have books by the ancient Greeks and Romans. So he had hundreds of old books copied out by hand in a style invented just for him, called Carolingian. Today, people are very glad he did because many books wouldn't have survived otherwise.

Books were so rare and precious in Charlemagne's day that they were chained to shelves and tables in the library. That way they weren't lost or stolen. Titles were written on the upper cover where they were easily seen. Later, when there were more books, they were stored upright, with the titles on their spines.

Today's libraries, like the Bibliothèque Nationale and the British Library, don't just collect millions of books. They also care for and repair them. Old books need special climate controls. They like the air dry and cool. Workshops full of people repair and restore broken or damaged books. Libraries are a book's best friend.

In every city and almost every small town, you'll find a library. In North America, there are 10 000 public libraries and another 6700 branch libraries, housing more than 1.5 billion books. Public libraries provide information and books to any-

## Memory Storehouse

In 1368, French king Charles V put together about 1000 manuscripts to make his own library. Now called the Bibliothèque Nationale, in Paris, France, it is a "storehouse for the world's memory." With its collection of more than 12 million volumes of printed books, as well as millions of periodicals, maps, prints, photographs, manuscripts, coins, medals, music documents, posters, scale models and others, it deserves that title. Perhaps the largest library in the world today is the British Library. It was begun in England by Sir Hans Sloane, a doctor and scientist who donated his books, manuscripts, coins, drawings and specimens of natural history to begin the British Museum. The Library today has 15 million printed books in it. But that's not all. It also has maps, stamps, recordings, newspapers— really anything to do with communication—for a total of about 150 million items.

## Autographs

Have you ever asked for someone's autograph? Imagine if you had your favorite rock singer or movie star's autograph on a piece of paper. Would that piece of paper be more important to you than the paper that you wrote your last spelling test on? Why? They're both just words written on a page. But people collect autographs because they think that the autograph somehow connects them to the person who wrote it. Although it's just dry ink on a page, it has a kind of magical importance. In fact, people who collect autographs sometimes pay a lot of money just to own the piece of paper that a famous person wrote on. In 1986, someone bought a letter at an auction because it had Thomas Jefferson's signature on it. (Thomas Jefferson was the president of the United States from 1801-1809.) The person paid a record $360 000 for that autograph.

one, free of charge. They can't keep every book ever published, but for most people, the local library has everything they need. And if your library doesn't have what you want, it can usually borrow it from another library.

Many libraries start small. Book lovers begin collecting books that they are interested in. Sometimes these collections grow to become libraries that can be used by other people. A rich American named Pierpont Morgan started a collection of autographs and stained glass when he was 13 years old. He simply began by writing to a few famous people to ask for their autographs. By the time he died in 1913, he had one of the world's largest private libraries. The Pierpont Morgan is now a public library and museum in New York City.

Why don't you start your own library collection? Are there any kinds of books that you are particularly interested in? Pierpont Morgan loved art, history and literature and his collection shows that. You can catalogue and arrange your books and share your library with your friends. Who knows? Maybe in years to come you'll have a famous collection, large enough to be made into a public library.

## The Power of the Pen

From toothpaste ads to the ingredients of your breakfast cereal to news from other countries—there's a lot of writing around today. Everywhere you turn, there's writing waiting to be read. It's hard to understand that there was a time when words were rare and to be obeyed.

Long ago, the only people who could write were the rich and powerful. Lawmakers used writing to set down the rules and regulations of the land. Priests wrote out religious laws and the ideas of their religious leaders. Writing told people how they should behave and what they should think. The actual, physical words on the page were sacred and respected objects. Written words had power.

Gradually, as more and more people learned how to read and write, others wrote down ideas and thoughts that were important to them. Aside from the laws of government and religion, scientists wrote down the physical laws of the universe. But sometimes, there were contradictions in the writings. People didn't always agree with each other.

Galileo was a scientist who lived in the 17th century. He spent his life studying how the planets moved. In 1632, he wrote a book called *Dialogue on the Great World Systems*, in which he explained that the earth moves around the sun. Today we know that Galileo was right. But in 1632, most people thought that the sun moved around the earth and that the earth did not move. This idea was very important to them. So when Galileo wrote his book, it created quite an uproar. Galileo was given a choice—either he could say that the book was a lie and that he didn't believe in what he'd written, or he would be executed. Galileo decided he'd rather live so he said that what he'd written was a lie. But under his breath he said to himself, "And yet it moves!" For Galileo, what he wrote or didn't write, what he believed or didn't believe, didn't alter the truth. The earth does move around the sun and it would, no matter what he said or wrote. But for the people who were against Galileo, his words were so dangerous that they had to be destroyed.

### PEN International

There are organizations that try to help people who have been put in jail for what they've written. One of these is a group called PEN International. The members of PEN write letters to governments all over the world, asking that they free writers in prison, or, at very least, stop torturing jailed writers. They also write letters to the people in prison to keep their spirits up. They are real PEN pals.

Getting rid of too-powerful writing still happens today. This is called censorship. There is an expression: "The pen is mightier than the sword." That means that writing can make more changes happen than fighting. Writing is a very powerful tool for changing the way people think. Because of this, people sometimes think there are certain ideas that are too dangerous for people to read.

Freedom of expression means that a person is able to write (or paint, draw, sculpt or film) whatever he or she wants. But sometimes other people disagree and will try to stop free expression. Books may be hidden away or burned so that people can't read them. Writers may be punished by being put into prisons or even killed. Some writers take that chance because they believe so strongly in the ideas they are writing about.

Sometimes people feel they need to protect their children from certain ideas or words. It's not that they want to burn books or punish authors, but they want certain books removed from schools and libraries. This is called challenging a book.

Books are most often challenged on the grounds of racism, morality, politics or obscenity. Sometimes challenged books are removed from the school or library shelves; other times they are not. The question of what books to have in a library and what books to teach in a school is a difficult one. Teachers and librarians try to decide on a policy for book selection. That means they decide on the type of information that they want the books to provide and why.

The next time you're in your school or public library, ask the librarians how they choose the books they put on the shelves. No one library could hold all the books ever published, so choices have to be made. Ask if you could look at a book catalogue. Looking at the books in there, how would you make your choices if you were the librarian?

## GRAFFITI

If you live in a city or even a small town, you've probably seen graffiti. The word "graffiti" comes from an Italian word that means scribbling or scratching. Graffiti is writing or pictures scrawled on walls or other unusual writing surfaces.

Graffiti can be a way of spreading ideas. Or it can simply be mischievous. Once, Irish theater manager James Daly bet a friend that he could invent a new word and make it the talk of the town in one day. That night, while everyone else was sleeping, he had friends paint his new word on walls throughout the town. The next morning, all anyone wanted to talk about was the word that they saw everywhere but didn't know the meaning of. The word was "quiz" and it came to mean "a test of knowledge."

Sometimes graffiti can be seen as a dangerous thing. In China in the 1970s, people were not supposed to write criticism of their government, or suggest that things might be done differently. Then someone put up a handwritten poster on a wall in Beijing that criticized the way the country was being run. People came to read the poster. Soon more and more posters went up and more and more people came to read them. No one signed a name to the posters—everything was anonymous. But the ideas were there. People thought; people talked about change. The posters were just words on a page but they were words that sparked ideas and hope.

Eventually the government in China stopped Democracy Wall, as it came to be called, by putting guards at the wall. The posters stopped going up. But the writing had made people realize that they were not alone in their thoughts, that other people wanted things to change, too.

# BLISS AND BRAILLE

Reading and writing is so important in people's lives that they will often struggle very hard to do it, even if it doesn't come easily. People who are blind cannot see to read or write. Braille is a written language for blind people based on touch rather than eyesight. It was invented by a man named Louis Braille who was blinded in an accident when he was three years old.

Braille writing consists of a series of raised dots. A six-dot pattern is used as a background for each letter of the alphabet. It looks like this ⠿ . A letter is written by using large dots within the pattern. For example, the letter B looks like this ⠿ . The large dots are raised off the surface of the page. People learn to read these raised dots with their fingertips.

a b c d e f g h i j
k l m n o p q r s t
u v w x y z

Try writing your own Braille sentence and learn to read it with your fingertips.

**You'll need:**
a dull pencil
construction paper
towels

1. Draw the dots of the letters you want to Braille on your page.

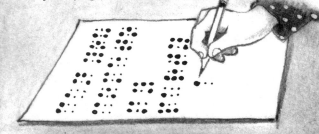

2. Turn the paper over so the writing is backwards. Re-draw the dots on this side.

3. Place your construction paper on a soft surface (your towels, folded up). Then gently press your pencil onto each large dot to form raised dots on the other side, trying not to make holes in the paper. To read your Braille writing, turn the page over and feel the raised dots. With practice, your fingers and brain will work together to read the dots, even when you have your eyes closed.

Can you figure out what this says? Answer on page 96.

Imagine if you could see and hear, but not talk. You would probably communicate with people by writing. But what if you couldn't hold a pen? There are some people who are not physically able to talk or hold a pen. They can understand what everyone is saying but can't communicate back. These people can sometimes use a written code called the Bliss System. With a Blissymbol board, which is a board of symbols that sits on a person's lap, they can point to a symbol or group of symbols to make their meaning understood. Here are some examples of Bliss Symbols:

food   drink   milk   happy   sad   good   bad

You can see how the symbols are using the same ideas in different ways.

# You Can Do It!

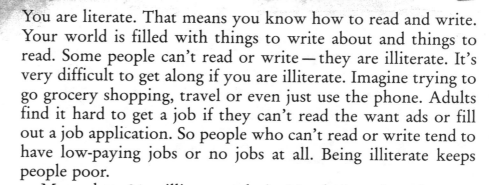

You are literate. That means you know how to read and write. Your world is filled with things to write about and things to read. Some people can't read or write — they are illiterate. It's very difficult to get along if you are illiterate. Imagine trying to go grocery shopping, travel or even just use the phone. Adults find it hard to get a job if they can't read the want ads or fill out a job application. So people who can't read or write tend to have low-paying jobs or no jobs at all. Being illiterate keeps people poor.

More than 24 million people in North America, almost 1 *billion* world-wide, are illiterate. Organizations such as the

United Nations, UNESCO and the Literacy Volunteers in your states and towns are working to erase illiteracy. They teach people around the world to read and write, and they send supplies, books and teachers to countries that can't afford them. Every day, people are learning to take control of their lives through reading and writing.

The ability to read and write is the key to all of the knowledge of the world. For more than 5000 years, people have enjoyed the ability to write down their thoughts and ideas. You, too, can be part of this great human tradition that knows no bounds of time and space. Pick up a pencil and Write On!

# GLOSSARY

**Broad-edged pen:** A pen that has a wide, flat writing end

**Calligraphy:** Beautiful writing. A calligrapher is someone who does calligraphy.

**Censorship:** The prohibition or banning of certain words or ideas

**Character:** A distinctive mark or sign from a writing system

**Codex:** A book that has pages bound together (like this one)

**Graphite:** A form of carbon (a soft rock) used for making pencils

**Ideogram:** A picture sign that stands for an idea or concept

**Illumination:** The art of decorating letters with colors and gold leaf

**Mnemonic device:** A memory aid; something that helps you to remember

**Offset printing:** A photographic printing method. With this method a photograph is chemically transferred onto a metal plate, which can then be used for printing.

**Papyrus:** A tall, rush-like plant; used for making a paper-like writing surface

**Parchment:** The skin of a goat or sheep prepared and used as a writing surface

**Petroglyphs:** Pictures and abstract designs carved or painted onto rock surfaces, usually cliffs

**Pictogram:** A picture sign that stands for a spoken word

**Phonogram:** A picture sign that stands for a sound

**Pulp:** A soft, wet mass of fiber, usually wood, used for making paper

**Scribe:** A person who writes by hand

**Spine:** The edge of a book where all of the pages are held together

**Syllabary:** A group of abstract signs that stand for the sounds in a spoken language

**Vellum:** The skin of a calf, prepared and used as a writing surface

# INDEX

# ANSWERS

*Egyptian Pictograms*, page 10
1 ox,  2 star,  3 water,  4 man,  5 road.

*International Symbols*, page 13
1 lost and found to the left,  2 lockers to the right,
3 elevators downstairs,  4 restaurant downstairs,
5 arrivals to the left and departures straight ahead,
6 men's and women's washrooms straight ahead,  7 taxi
and bus stop to the right.

*Rebus Puzzle*, page 14
part + tea  = party
eye + knot = why not

*Letter Puzzles*, page 19
1d, 2e, 3b, 4a, 5c.

*Writing Systems*, page 21
Chinese writing is based on picture writing. Chinese is
the oldest, continuous non-alphabetic writing system in
the world.

*How Many As*, page 67
There are 147 As in the text on this page. Multiply that
by 96 pages and you get 14 112.

*Type Designs*, page 69
Numbers 1 and 4 have serifs. Numbers 2 and 3 are sans-
serif type designs.

*Braille*, page 91
The phrase BOOKS ARE FOR EVERYBODY is
spelled out in Braille.